"Only a Paper Moon"
The Theatre of Billy Rose

Theater and Dramatic Studies, No. 42

Oscar G. Brockett, Series Editor

Leslie Waggener Professor of Fine Arts
and Professor of Drama
The University of Texas at Austin

Other Titles in This Series

No. 33	*The Dance Theatre of Jean Cocteau*	Frank W. D. Ries
No. 34	*No Man's Stage: A Semiotic Study of Jean Genet's Major Plays*	Una Chaudhuri
No. 35	*The Drama Review: Thirty Years of Commentary on the Avant-Garde*	Brooks McNamara and Jill Dolan, eds.
No. 36	*Political Violence in Drama: Classical Models, Contemporary Variations*	Mary Karen Dahl
No. 37	*Peter Weiss in Exile: A Critical Study of His Works*	Roger Ellis
No. 39	*The Wooster Group, 1975–1985: Breaking the Rules*	David Savran
No. 40	*Late Victorian Farce*	Jeffrey H. Huberman
No. 41	*Shakespeare at the Maddermarket: Nugent Monck and the Norwich Players*	Franklin J. Hildy

"Only a Paper Moon"
The Theatre of Billy Rose

by
Stephen Nelson

UMI Research Press
Ann Arbor, Michigan

Copyright © 1987, 1985
Stephen Nelson
All rights reserved

Produced and distributed by
UMI Research Press
an imprint of
University Microfilms, Inc.
Ann Arbor, Michigan 48106

Library of Congress Cataloging in Publication Data

Nelson, Stephen, 1952-
 "Only a paper moon."

  (Theater and dramatic studies ; no. 42)
  Revision of the author's thesis (Ph.D.)—New York
University, 1985.
   Bibliography: p.
   Includes index.
   1. Rose, Billy, 1899-1966. 2. Theatrical producers
and directors—United States—Biography. I. Title.
II. Series.
PN2287.R756N4 1987   792'.0232'0924 [B]   87-5001
ISBN 0-8357-1796-8 (alk. paper)

For my father, Robert Nelson

Contents

List of Figures   *ix*

Preface   *xiii*

1 "Mr. Fanny Brice"   *1*

2 "Broadway Billy"   *13*

3 *Jumbo*   *29*

4 Fort Worth   *47*

5 Cleveland, 1937: The First *Aquacade*   *63*

6 Nightclubs, 1938–1951   *79*

7 World's Fairs, 1939–1940   *97*

8 The War and After   *119*

Notes   *143*

Bibliography   *159*

Index   *163*

List of Figures

1. Mayor Jimmy Walker Marries Billy Rose and Fanny Brice, 1929   *12*

2. Arthur Treacher and Fanny Brice in *Sweet and Low*, 1930   *18*

3. James Barton and Fanny Brice in *Sweet and Low*, 1930   *18*

4. Flyer for Casino de Paree   *26*

5. Flyer for the Billy Rose Music Hall   *27*

6. Circus Ring for *Jumbo*, New York Hippodrome, 1935   *34*

7. Catwalk for *Jumbo*, New York Hippodrome, 1935   *35*

8. Jimmy Durante in *Jumbo*, New York Hippodrome, 1935   *37*

9. Act 1 Finale of *Jumbo*, New York Hippodrome, 1935   *43*

10. Finale of *Jumbo*, New York Hippodrome, 1935   *44*

11. Model of Theatre in Casa Mañana, Fort Worth, 1936   *54*

12. Audience as Seen from the Stage in Casa Mañana, Fort Worth, 1936   *55*

13. *The Last Frontier*, Fort Worth, 1936   *56*

14. The Sunset Trail, Fort Worth, 1936   *57*

15. *Aquacade* Amphitheatre, Great Lakes Exposition, 1937   *69*

x   List of Figures

16. Advertisement for Cleveland *Aquacade*, 1937   *72*

17. Scene from Cleveland *Aquacade*, 1937   *73*

18. "Half and Half," Number from Cleveland *Aquacade*, 1937   *75*

19. Finale of Cleveland *Aquacade*, 1937   *76*

20. Palm Beach Bar, Casa Mañana, New York, 1938   *82*

21. Sally Rand and Oscar Shaw in *Let's Play Fair*, 1938   *85*

22. Interior of the Diamond Horseshoe, ca. 1940   *89*

23. Scenes from Diamond Horseshoe Revues, ca. 1948   *92*

24. Opening Scene from the *Aquacade*, 1939 New York World's Fair   *104*

25. Beach Ball Scene from the *Aquacade*, 1939 New York World's Fair   *105*

26. Roller Skating Scene from the *Aquacade*, 1939 New York World's Fair   *106*

27. Johnny Weissmuller, 1939   *108*

28. *Aquacade* Publicity Stunt, 1939 New York World's Fair   *109*

29. *Aquacade* Publicity Stunt, 1939 New York World's Fair   *110*

30. *Aquacade* Advertisement, 1939 New York World's Fair Souvenir Program   *111*

31. Salvador Dali's *Dream of Venus*, New York World's Fair, 1940   *112*

32. *Aquacade*, 1940 Golden Gate International Exposition   *116*

33. Finale of *Aquacade*, 1940 Golden Gate International Exposition   *117*

34. Scene from the New York Production of *The Fifth Column,* 1940   *121*

35. Scene from the New York Production of *We Will Never Die,* 1943   *125*

36. Scenes from the 1943 New York Production of *Carmen Jones*   *130*

37. Beatrice Lillie and Bert Lahr in "Fragonard" from the New York Production of *Seven Lively Arts*   *134*

38. Geraldine Page and Louis Jourdan in the 1954 New York Production of *The Immoralist*   *138*

Preface

This study chronicles the stage productions of the late Billy Rose, an American impresario active in the commercial theatre from 1924 to 1962. Although Rose's public personality has received a great deal of attention, there has been almost no analysis of the fascinating theatrical legacy he left behind. This work will attempt to rectify that by examining Rose's productions in detail and divining the thread that links them to one another and to the larger tradition of American popular entertainment. Billy Rose's character, both as a person and as a producer, makes an examination of his work difficult. With some artists, the course of their creative lives follows a discernable pattern of development and evolutionary change. In Rose's case, however, sequence is practically nonexistent.

Rose began his adult life as a stenographer and started writing song lyrics in his early twenties. His experience writing for musicals and revues prompted an interest in producing. After several of his songs became commercial successes, he went into the nightclub business, and produced his first show in 1930. For the next thirty years he was involved in a variety of productions from straight plays and Broadway musicals to spectacles, cabaret shows and world's fair amusements. The breadth of his interests provides us an opportunity to examine many of the significant trends in twentieth-century American show business.

Rose created a style of theatre that was as unique as it was outlandish. His ability to mix elements from such disparate sources as circuses, nightclubs, vaudeville, musical comedy, aquatics and burlesque resulted in productions of a scale and sumptuousness seldom equaled in the commercial theatre. It was a style that was of the theatre and yet outside it; for while Rose owed a great debt to earlier purveyors of theatrical spectacle (such as Bolossy and Imre Kiralfy, Florenz Ziegfeld and Hassard Short), he was also very much a part of the outdoor amusement tradition (as exemplified by showmen such as P. T. Barnum and Frederic Thompson and Elmer Dundy, the founders of Coney Island's Luna Park).

The impetus for this project grew out of several years of research on world's fairs and spectacle performance. In examining the many significant expositions of the 1930s, I found it hard to ignore Billy Rose's influence on the amusement environments at those fairs and on the overall character of the expositions themselves. The great diversity of popular entertainments and theatrical productions that bore his name prompted further inquiry. It seemed likely that so famous and prolific a producer would have been well covered by theatre scholars, if for no other reason than that his name was affixed to one of the nation's most important and extensive theatre collections (the Billy Rose Theatre Collection, housed at the New York Public Library at Lincoln Center).

Surprisingly, I discovered that there was no critical study of any phase of his work. The two published books on Rose, *The Nine Lives of Billy Rose* by his sister Polly Rose Gottlieb, and Earl Conrad's *Manhattan Primitive,* are essentially anecdotal reminiscences and deal only briefly with his productions. There is a dissertation on the career of Rose's chief director John Murray Anderson, but it offers only a cursory examination of Anderson's role in Rose's productions. Anderson's own memoirs, *Out without My Rubbers,* provide an interesting and useful account of his twenty-year working relationship with Billy Rose.

The book is arranged chronologically, with each chapter focusing on particular productions or entertainments. Since the thrust of the study is Rose's theatrical career, there is only a brief discussion of his activities as a songwriter, columnist and art collector. His frequently flamboyant personal life cannot be completely ignored, but it has been covered extensively by others and is discussed here only to the extent that it relates to specific aspects of Rose's involvement with the theatre or popular entertainment.

I would like to thank Brooks McNamara and my wife Susan for their help and support in the preparation of this work.

1

"Mr. Fanny Brice"

Billy Rose was one of the most flamboyant and controversial personalities in twentieth-century American theatre. Throughout his forty-year career he earned both lavish praise and unbridled hatred, often from the same people. He was, to say the least, a paradox: a moody dreamer who projected an image of ruthless arrogance, an intensely private man who lived for notoriety. Even in the world of show business, few men ever sought and relished publicity to such a degree.

Rose seemed to need enemies, and often cultivated opponents the way some men nurture friendships. He was fiercely contentious and yet longed for acceptance and respect. Hundreds of people knew him, but no one professed to understand him: he could be sincere and devious in the same breath. Yet, whatever one thought of Billy Rose, it was impossible to be indifferent to him. On that point at least, there is little question.

Rose's career in the theatre emerged from a background that was both unlikely and appropriate. He was born William S. Rosenberg on September 6, 1899, in a tenement on Manhattan's Lower East Side. Rose claimed to have been born on the kitchen table, a reasonable possibility given the Rosenberg family's cramped living quarters. He also maintained that he was born the day William McKinley was shot, in part to support his oft repeated joke that "Most people on Broadway will tell you they shot the wrong man."[1] McKinley was in fact shot on September 6, but two years after Rose's birth.

About the Rosenbergs' unfortunate circumstances, there is little doubt. Fanny and David Rosenberg came to the United States to escape a pogram in western Russia. Their perilous economic situation was typical of many Eastern European Jews forced to immigrate to America at the turn of the century. The building on Allen Street in which Rose was born was designed to hold sixteen families. In reality, there were usually between forty and forty-five families living there at any one time. Fanny Rosenberg soon resolved to find a better place to raise her children.

She was a capable and determined woman whose yearning for the good life contrasted sharply with her husband's laconic acceptance of the status quo. Despite David's lack of motivation, Fanny managed to move the family to a better neighborhood in the Bronx when Billy was five. Over the next several years, the Rosenbergs lived at numerous addresses in the Bronx and Manhattan. By the time Rose entered the High School of Commerce, he had attended eight different New York City schools.

Family hardship is often thought to have sparked Rose's craving for recognition. In reality, the deprivations of childhood were more important to him in later life—a convenient rags-to-riches story he often told from the comfortable perspective of his Beekman Place brownstone. In fact, Billy Rose the showman owed far more to his high school shorthand championships and a job as Bernard Baruch's secretary during World War I. For while poverty was his point of origin, the ways of the powerful and privileged shaped Rose's view of the world and his place in it.

As with many events in his life, Rose's tenure with Baruch was a combination of luck and hustle. From the very beginning Rose had a propensity for being in the right place at the right time. His shorthand skills first came to the attention of an Irishman named John Gregg, who was trying to sell his new shorthand method to the New York City Board of Education. Certain that his system would prove superior to the established Pitman shorthand, Gregg convinced city school officials to allow him to experiment with the new technique at the High School of Commerce in Manhattan. The school was known primarily for its emphasis on typing, accounting and other office skills.

When Gregg began his program of shorthand classes in 1915, Rose was enrolled in a Pitman class. He switched to the Gregg Shorthand Club after some persuasive lobbying by Gregg's instructors, who kept their eyes out for promising students. Their goal was to enter Gregg's protégés in local and national competitions against Pitman students as proof of the Gregg system's superiority.

The opportunity first arose in 1917 at a citywide high school competition known as the Metropolitan Contest. Rose won his first major shorthand title by taking dictation at a record-setting 160 words a minute, with an accuracy of nearly ninety-nine percent. Even more remarkable were the circumstances surrounding the triumph. A few days prior to the contest, Rose had sprained his wrist skating in Central Park. The swelling was so bad that his fingers would not close around a pen. He solved the problem by carving a hole in a potato and securing a pen in it. Gripping the vegetable with his half-closed hand, Rose was able to write well enough to win first prize.[2]

Such perseverance was not lost on John Gregg. When the war forced the cancellation of the national shorthand competition in 1918, Gregg offered Rose a job as his private secretary. Although the job paid the substantial sum of seventy-five dollars a week, Rose soon became restless. Living at home with his parents and two sisters and working for Gregg in Yaphank, New Jersey was hardly paradise for a seventeen-year-old with Billy Rose's ambitions. When he encountered a newspaper advertisement seeking stenographers for the War Industries Board in Washington, he jumped at the chance.[3]

Always mindful of opportunity, Rose soon realized that board chairman Bernard Baruch was the man to work for. After studying Baruch's work habits, Rose learned that his boss was troubled by the seeming impossibility of obtaining a complete record of the numerous meetings he attended each day. When Rose proposed to hand him a prepared text of his every conversation by nine o'clock the same evening, Baruch was intrigued and took a chance on the proposition. It was an early example of the tireless self-promotion and relentless need to impress people that would become hallmarks of Rose's theatrical career.

As Baruch's personal stenographer, Rose made good on his promise and soon had fellow shorthand experts from the High School of Commerce ensconced in the steno pool. In later years, Rose's press agents inflated his work at the board, making him into an unsung war hero and Baruch's closest confidant. But Rose did strike up a friendship with the older man, who soon became a kind of surrogate father. Years later in a radio broadcast, Rose talked about his relationship with Baruch:

> I think he was attracted to me because he quickly sensed that I admired him, that I was devoted to him.... He was the best looking man in North America, as far as I was concerned. He wore the quietest and best-fitting clothes, he was pink-skinned, prematurely gray.... He was a living legend when he was forty-eight. I got stuck on him and I guess the old boy found it attractive.[4]

That Rose saw Baruch as a father figure was not surprising, given his own father's personality. David Rosenberg was hardly a model of parental responsibility; he seemed unable to hold either a steady job or any genuine affection for his family. His wife Fanny raised the children and made most important family decisions. Where David was unmotivated, she was driven. While her husband seemed profoundly uninterested in the family, Fanny made it her life. She adored her son and placed on him all the expectations her husband never fulfilled. The shorthand success was just the beginning, she told David. Billy would make a name for himself. She knew it.

Baruch introduced Rose to the machinations of powerful men and the world in which they moved. Toward the end of Rose's six-month stint at the board, Baruch asked him to deliver a letter to President Wilson. Wilson's secretary told Rose that the president would like to see him. Wilson, it seemed, knew shorthand and had heard from Baruch of Rose's phenomenal speed. The president, who had learned the Pitman system, was anxious to compare his talents with those of the young expert. For a quarter of an hour the two tested each other at dictation. Wilson was apparently pleased when Rose complimented him on his accuracy and speed. They exchanged shorthand notes as a souvenir of the occasion and Rose left feeling quite accomplished for a nervous seventeen-year-old.[5]

When the war ended, Rose had a little extra money and no clear idea of what to do next. It is here that the record becomes muddy, for Rose himself is the only source. Although the details vary depending on when and to whom he told them, the essential event was a chance meeting with a young actress. Rose had taken what little savings he had at the war's end and embarked on a trip across America. He ran short of funds in New Orleans and decided to return to New York by boat. One of the passengers was an aspiring actress named Edna Harris, with whom Rose managed to strike up a friendship. When the ship docked, he made arrangements to see her in New York.[6]

While his brief liaison with Harris is often seen as prompting Rose's turn to show business, there were other factors as well. When he returned to New York, Rose again went to work for John Gregg, who began grooming him for the 1919 National Shorthand Competition. As practice for the upcoming contest, Rose and many of Gregg's other students went to Keith's Vaudeville several times a week and took down the lyrics and routines they heard. He soon developed a liking for popular entertainment that had much to do with the abrupt end of his shorthand career.

The national contest was held in Detroit where Rose shared a hotel room with Harry Rapaport, Gregg's other entry in the competition. The night before the championship, the two boys decided to go for an outing and asked if there were any theatres in the area. The hotel bellhop informed them that the real action was across the river in Windsor, where local revelers went to escape the state of Michigan's three-year ban on liquor.

To a couple of teenagers from the Lower East Side, the place seemed a veritable Babylon. Dozens of loud, brightly lit saloons and cabarets lined the streets crowded with tipsy Detroiters. Signs proclaimed, "Welcome Americans!" After regaling bar patrons with samples of their shorthand prowess and earning numerous free drinks, the young men staggered back to their hotel. For two strait-laced Jewish boys it was quite a night. For Rose, it was the first time he had ever gotten drunk.

The next morning in the midst of the competition, Rose suddenly stopped, slid from his chair and passed out with a hangover. Efforts to revive him in time failed. For the first time, Billy Rose had let an opportunity slip away. Rose never again entered a shorthand competition or took a job as a stenographer. He also never drank again, even as one of the most successful nightclub owners in New York.[7]

After the Detroit fiasco, Rose saw more of the young actress he met on the boat. Edna introduced Rose to the haunts of the theatre crowd, one of the more prominent of which was Wolpin's, an inauspicious delicatessen frequented primarily by songwriters. Here Tin Pan Alley types gathered to talk shop, gossip and consume large glasses of celery tonic and plates of pastrami and boiled cabbage. They were a disheveled and frantic group who smoked too much, talked loud and kept extremely odd hours. They certainly did not appear to young Rose to be a particularly wealthy or powerful lot, at least not by the standards he had seen in Washington. He was startled to learn from Edna that even the moderately successful among them occasionally earned upwards of $2000 a week. "How come so many of them look like bums?" Rose inquired, "What do they do with it all?"[8] He soon found out.

The period immediately after the First World War was a time of great turmoil in New York, but it was an opportune chaos for those able to exploit it. The public was hungry for entertainment and escape after the trauma of war. The crunch of returning servicemen, refugees and fortune seekers that crowded Manhattan's streets in 1919 and 1920 provided both a ready labor pool and a burgeoning market for the right diversion at the right price.

The songwriters Rose encountered in Wolpin's, Lindy's and other hangouts were desperately trying to supply music publishers, producers, singers and other purveyors of popular songs with the raw material of success. Commercial radio and records were just beginning to reach a large audience, and with a "piano in every parlor" still the rule in much of the country, catchy tunes could spread like wildfire. The key was getting the song heard by the right people and played for the right audience. The promotion and management of a song required a persistence and drive that most songwriters lacked.

Rose knew that the few really clever songwriters, the ones who stayed on top and commanded respect, were shrewd businessmen who not only understood clever tunes and phrases, but also grasped the economic structure of the music business. They were the survivors, and with what little he knew of their world in 1920, Rose knew that they were the ones to follow and learn from. Above all else, Billy Rose was a survivor. The game was new, but it was just a matter of learning the rules and the important players, of finding the angle, the opening, the weakness. He had done it before with shorthand. He would do it again.

Through Edna, Rose met a host of others seeking to gain entrance to the world of show business. The pool halls and all-night diners were full of actors, singers and writers-to-be trying to edge their way into what looked like a gold mine. Rose struck up a friendship with an out-of-work actor named George Raft who liked his bright chatter and talent for the quick joke, something the taciturn Raft lacked. The two also shared a fondness for billiards; Raft was a pool shark and looked it. Rose also shot well, but did not look it. The combination proved profitable, with Rose posing as bait to draw a sucker into a game.

The pool hustle gave Rose a closer look at the songwriters whose earning power he envied, but whose loose and careless manner with money astounded him. They would often drop several hundred dollars on a pool game and shrug it off as "easy come, easy go." The easy come of it all began to appeal to Rose, who desperately needed a way out of the pool halls. Songwriting might just be the answer.

One evening in Lindy's, Rose noted that, although the restaurant was completely packed, a prime corner table was conspicuously empty. George Raft informed him that it was reserved for the most successful songwriters, those with yearly incomes in six figures. In the months that followed Rose watched that table and the people who sat there. He would overhear tales of how this tune or that was tossed out in no time and had brought its writer riches. He sized up the big talkers at the sacred table and decided that they were nothing special. "How come they're making all this money?" he asked Raft. "I don't see lightning coming out of their ears. If they can do it, I can do it."[9]

So Billy Rose set out to become a songwriter. As with all his endeavors, he approached this one with a methodical, almost obsessive thoroughness. Already familiar with the social environment and personalities of the business, Rose decided to acquaint himself with the mechanics of songwriting. His lack of musical background and training made lyric writing the only practical avenue to follow. He began a cram course in the history of the popular song, studying lyrics and looking closely at the most frequently used subjects and rhymes.

Rose spent long hours at the Forty-second Street Library poring over song books and lyric sheets. For weeks he constructed elaborate consonant and vowel charts to isolate the sounds and rhythm patterns that separated hit songs from duds. At night he often sat huddled with a scratch pad at a deli counter, trying to come up with his own hits. Despite his diligence, the words did not always come forth in a torrent of inspiration. One night in Wolpin's Rose asked composer Harry Ruby, "Has anyone ever thought of rhyming June with macaroon?" The entire delicatessen applauded. A waiter handed him a pencil and a clean menu and said, "Mr. Rose, you're in business."[10]

Perhaps nothing in Rose's career is more open to question and controversy than his success as a songwriter. Many have suggested that he simply took the work of others and affixed his name to it. There was little doubt that his chief talent was motivating and organizing the efforts of his less headstrong colleagues. As Harry Warren, one of Rose's principal coauthors, noted, "Billy could be cruel, but he was a great feeder. He'd sit with the boys and say, 'Now come on, you can do better than that.'... He stimulated the real lyricists to produce."[11]

Rose made a habit of keeping an eye out for talented lyricists. His secret lay not only in finding good collaborators, but also in selling the finished product. Rose's association with Al Dubin and Mort Dixon was typical of the way he worked. Dubin and Dixon had written lyrics for Victor Herbert's *Indian Summer* of 1919, and Dixon had penned most of the words for the immensely popular "That Old Gang of Mine." Their problem came from a shared tendency to rely on the bottle for inspiration. Along with their drinking proclivities went a certain lack of business sense and none of the drive needed to promote and publish a popular song. Rose saw to it that Dubin and Dixon were well supplied with both liquor and the necessary motivation.

They came to Rose's Seventh Avenue apartment where he plied them with drinks, jokes and cigarettes until they seemed ready to roll. Then he would pull out song titles, phrases and ideas until Dubin and Dixon found something they could work with. Once a lyric was hammered out, Rose went out and found someone to do the music. He ran the process like an assembly line, sometimes working with a dozen writers on ten or more songs at a time. He was equally adept at getting material accepted by publishers, something few songwriters seemed able to do as well as the aggressive Rose. As Harry Warren remembers, Rose soon had a reputation for being able to get a song sold and come up with a quick advance. "You waited outside while Billy was in there bludgeoning an advance out of the publisher.... Not until you got a statement did you learn what he sold the song for."[12]

No one seemed immune to the Rose technique. His reputation in Tin Pan Alley soon became larger than life. He was always taking shorthand notes in restaurants, in the theatre, whenever he had an idea or heard one he liked. "Beware of his shorthand. It's longer than you think," was one oft repeated caveat. In explaining how Rose's name appeared with his as colyricist for "Cheerful Little Earful," Ira Gershwin responded, "He came in one day and made a suggestion about changing a line.... I didn't feel like fighting."[13]

Yet despite his heavy reliance on the genius of others, Rose's imprint on most of his songs is unmistakable. "It was the way he talked," Chester Conn said of songs like "Barney Google" and "I Found a Million Dollar Baby in a Five and Ten Cent Store." "That was the language he used in his daily discourse."[14] Nowhere is the Rose touch more evident than in the one song for which he is given undisputed credit, a jingle that was one of the first singing commercials:

> Does the Spearmint lose its flavor on the bedpost overnight?
> If you paste it on the left side, will you find it on the right?
> Would you use it on your collar when your button's not in sight?
> Does the Spearmint lose its flavor on the bedpost overnight?[15]

Although he was now enjoying a fair degree of success, Rose wanted more. While his aggressive methods had made him and his cronies a lot of money, it did not allow them to share in the fame and recognition that their songs generated for those who produced and performed them. With the exception of Irving Berlin and a handful of others, songwriters simply did not have the status accorded similarly accomplished actors, singers, directors and producers. Neither Rose, Dubin, Dixon, Warren nor the others could command the prestige and reverence of an Al Jolson, a Fanny Brice or a Florenz Ziegfeld. The best the songwriter could hope for was a good table at Lindy's, and for Billy Rose, that simply was not enough.

In June of 1924 Rose happened to notice that a marquee at the Ritz Theatre featured the name of an old acquaintance, Harry McCrae Webster, as director. The show was *The Fatal Wedding,* a classic melodrama written in 1893 by Gussie Davis, the era's first successful black composer.[16] It told the woeful tale of a wedding interrupted by the groom's first wife, who enters with a screaming baby in her arms. Things go from bad to worse as the baby dies, the husband commits suicide, and the two women become friends to shoulder their mutual grief. In the late nineteenth century, people had their handkerchiefs out for the entire evening's performance.[17]

The intervening years had brought about a somewhat less maudlin public sensibility, and *The Fatal Wedding* was now presented as a comedy that poked fun at the sentiments of an earlier day. It was both nostalgia for a simpler time and a satire designed for an audience of self-styled sophisticates. The reviews were good, but somehow the show was barely surviving at the box office. Rose went backstage to see Webster, and the director invited him to see the show. It was funny. Knowing of the show's meager business, Rose asked Webster to introduce him to the producer, a neophyte named Mary Kirkpatrick.

While there is no clear agreement as to how he managed it, Rose soon had an interest in the show and ultimately came to own the production.[18] He passed out tickets to songwriting cohorts and publicized the show until the box office began to improve. *The Fatal Wedding* continued on Broadway for several months and made Rose a good deal of money. It also showed him the appeal of entertainment that mixed nostalgia, satire and comedy. It was a combination he would employ again and again over the years.[19]

With proceeds from *The Fatal Wedding* and the growing royalties from "Barney Google" and other songs, Rose decided to go into the nightclub business, because, as he put it, "I wanted to wear a black hat and meet some girls."[20] The real reasons were a good deal more complex. He had always known that songwriting was a difficult business with no guarantee of a steady income. A club represented not only the security of real estate, but also (by serving liquor) the potential of a regular cash flow. Most important, for the notoriety-hungry Rose, it offered a way into the glamorous world of show business society that normally remained closed to songwriters.

The club was a tiny firetrap located over a garage on Fifty-sixth Street near Sixth Avenue, which Rose opened in November 1924 for an initial outlay of $4,000.[21] He called it the Backstage Club and decorated the interior accordingly. "He had the joint rigged out like the backstage of a theater. You stepped into the place over some footlights," recounted Max Arronsen, a Manhattan saloonkeeper who was an underworld notable at the time. "Rose always had this theater bug in him, and he thought this would appeal to the showbiz crowd."[22] Apparently it did.

Rose recovered his initial investment within a week. There was a band and a young singer from Danville, Illinois named Helen Morgan. When the club became so crowded that extra tables were placed over the dance floor, Rose told Morgan to sit on the piano. The pose became her trademark, and Morgan went on to became one of the country's most popular vocalists.[23] The Backstage Club soon became a favorite haunt of show business personalities from Sophie Tucker to Walter Winchell. The success of Rose's venture did not go unnoticed by another group of celebrities in New York, one that had a great interest in any establishment that sold bootleg liquor.

Soon after Rose's speakeasy opened, an emissary from the underworld came to see him with an offer of partnership. Rose curtly informed the man that he was not interested. The next night the club was raided and most of its liquor destroyed. The following evening, the mobster returned with his offer and received the same response. After a few more evenings of police whistles and broken bottles, Rose decided it might be advantageous to hear what the man in the outsized overcoat had to say. The heavy turned out to be Max Arronsen, who was then in the employ of Arnold Rothstein, a kingpin of the underworld. Arronsen convinced Rose that Rothstein should become a partner, and handed Rose a thousand dollars in cash. Although he often made twice as much on a good night, Rose saw the handwriting on the wall and gave in.[24]

Although Rothstein was one of the most powerful gangsters in the city, he did not fit the mold of such thug types as Dutch Shultz and Vincent "Mad Dog" Coll. Rothstein was a teetotaler who wore impeccably tailored suits and appeared to all the world like another successful businessman. He had financed Anne Nichols's *Abie's Irish Rose,* and considered anything in the vicinity of Broadway to be his territory.[25] In many respects he was an underworld Baruch, who saw young Rose as someone to whom he could dispense advice. Much of the counsel involved investment in bogus stock deals, narcotics and bootlegging. It was dangerous business, and in 1928 Rothstein was gunned down by an overzealous associate. Rose learned a great deal from Rothstein about nightclubs and the liquor business, but he also saw the limitations of operating too far outside the law. Although Max Arronsen and some of Rothstein's other cronies remained in Rose's circle for years afterwards, Rose soon realized the dangers inherent in partnership with the underworld.

The popularity of the Backstage Club convinced Rose that the public had money to burn and that he could see more of it in a venture that did not include gangsters. In 1926 Rose put $50,000 into the renovated second story of a Fifth Avenue mansion and christened the place the Fifth Avenue Club.[26] As befitted the establishment's posh locale, Rose instituted a five-dollar minimum on the theory that the first rule of exclusivity is to overcharge. To keep underworld interest low, he decided to serve no liquor, assuming that anyone who could afford to get in would probably have a ready supply of booze. He got two recent Columbia graduates named Richard Rodgers and Lorenz Hart to write a revue for the club's opening, entitled *Billy Rose's Sins of 1926*. The lyrics of the opening song gave a clue to the flavor of the evening and Rose's concept of entertainment:

> Kind gentlefolk you gaze upon a most unholy trinity,
> Compared to us Boccacio's a Doctor of Divinity,
> Our sins if laid from end to end would stretch into infinity,
> We earn an honest living while we rob you of your sleep.[27]

Some of the Fifth Avenue Club's more established neighbors were also being deprived of their rest, as Rose noted in a reminiscence of the club's opening night. "John D. [Rockefeller] was at the age when he needed his sleep something fierce, and when my bug-eyed musicians erupted with "Somebody Stole My Gal" at four in the morning, he hollered copper at the top of his ancient lungs."[28] Within five minutes two dozen police and three paddy wagons arrived at the club. Fortunately for Rose, the authorities simply warned him to mute his trumpets.

The police probably missed one of the show's high points, which featured a chorus routine with 190-pound showgirls. When Rose learned that Lee and J. J. Shubert were planning a number for their new show that included 200-pound girls, he cried foul. Although his lawyer solemnly informed him that fat girls were not a copyrightable commodity, Rose was fixed on revenge. Soon after the Shubert show *The Great Temptation* opened, Rose hired a dozen men and bought them tickets in various parts of the house. As the curtain went up, the men, dressed like bums, raised a commotion and threw cards around the theatre that bore the admonishment "Jake Shubert, Shame On You!" in large type followed by Rose's charge that his chubby chorine idea had been stolen.

Rose soon learned that few ideas in the theatre remained anyone's exclusive property. For someone who regularly appropriated other people's material in the songwriting business, Rose's outrage at the Shubert's routine smacked of the pot calling the kettle black. Rose apparently saw little irony in it and later noted, "Yep, I've only learned one thing from the Shuberts—how to add and subtract."[29]

Although *Billy Rose's Sins of 1926* starred Betty Compton and Constance Carpenter in addition to the plump chorus, the Fifth Avenue Club was not to be an overnight sensation like the Backstage Club. The stylish crowd Rose hoped to attract wanted somewhere they could drink; without alcohol the crowds soon disappeared. He managed to sell the place to a bootlegger after convincing the man's girlfriend to quit running a speakeasy and become a featured attraction. "Advertise yourself as a 'Mistress of Conversation,'" Rose advised the woman. "All the great women have done it. DuBarry, Pompadour, Marie Antoinette.... Wear a stylish gown and when the customers arrive—just talk to them. It'll be tremendous."[30]

Despite large ads billing his beloved as a "Mistress of Conversation," the bootlegger had little success with the Fifth Avenue Club. Few customers were enthralled with his girlfriend's discursive skills. Several weeks after he acquired the establishment, it went out of business.

From Rose's point of view, one of the principal benefits of nightclub ownership was the patronage of celebrities. Walter Winchell wrote frequently of the Backstage Club in his columns, thus insuring a regular cast of notables. One evening in the fall of 1926, Fanny Brice appeared and asked to meet the owner. Brice, who was then starring in the Ziegfeld Follies, was familiar with Rose's exploits as a lyricist and was particularly taken with a line from "In the Middle of the Night" that went, "in the middle of a moment, you and I forgot what no meant." Although by some accounts their initial meeting was less than love at first sight, Rose sensed a certain potential and pursued it with his usual zeal.[31]

Brice had recently divorced her gangster husband Nicky Arnstein, who was completing a prison term for fraud and forgery. Their marriage had produced two children and a desire on her part for a more stable relationship. In any event Brice seemed receptive to Rose's suggestion that he write her a vaudeville act. During the show's out-of-town tryouts, the two realized that, as Rose put it, "we liked the same jokes and disliked the same people."[32] Rose turned friendship into courtship with his typical proclivity for headline grabbing. In 1927, with Brice in Hollywood making a movie, Rose had himself flown from New York to California in an open-cockpit mail plane, an event columnists heralded as the first coast-to-coast romance of the airplane age.

While Rose may not have been entirely cynical in his pursuit of Brice, he was certainly aware of the benefits her affection would bring. She was his ticket to realms normally beyond the reach of saloon owners and Tin Pan Alley songwriters. Brice's wit and engaging personality made her home on East Sixty-ninth Street a frequent spot for parties that included Vanderbilts, Wanamakers and Astors, as well as the usual show business luminaries. It was a world Rose had glimpsed from a distance as Baruch's secretary and now had the chance to experience as a participant. It was an opportunity he could not pass up.

12 "Mr. Fanny Brice"

Figure 1. Mayor Jimmy Walker Marries Billy Rose and Fanny Brice, 1929
(Courtesy Billy Rose Theatre Collection, New York Public Library, Astor, Lenox and Tilden Foundations)

On February 8, 1929, Billy Rose and Fanny Brice were married at City Hall with Mayor Jimmy Walker officiating. Just before the ceremony, Rose turned to Walker and said, "I'll give you a dollar now and the other dollar if it's a success."[33] The photograph of the occasion is particularly revealing (fig. 1). Rose's steely-eyed smirk calls to mind a big game hunter who has just bagged a prize trophy. Soon, however, Rose began to wonder just whose head was on the wall. Entrance into Brice's world carried a high price, and he soon became "that saloon owner who married Fanny Brice," or more simply, "Mr. Fanny Brice." He was the butt of such jokes as: "What's Billy Rose up to?" Answer: "My waist."

Still it was a stigma he was more than willing to endure for the many advantages the marriage provided. He had learned that songwriters seldom held the spotlight indefinitely. Sooner or later their fame and wealth slipped away while the real money and power stayed where they always were—with producers. Producers always commanded respect and attention, always seemed to be at the center of things. They were the ones the stars played up to. There was no doubt about it: the only way to eliminate Mr. Brice was for Mr. Rose to become a producer.

2
"Broadway Billy"

That Rose should choose a revue to make his producing debut is not surprising. As with many terms in the theatre, "revue" has meant different things at different times, and producers have often employed it to add a dash of flair and sophistication to their shows.[1] It was a form ideally suited to someone with Rose's talents and tastes. His songwriting and cabaret experiences had already revealed a penchant for things topical and flamboyant. He also seemed to have an unusual sense of what struck the public fancy.

The *Encyclopedia Britannica* defines revue as "a light form of theatrical entertainment deriving from the French street fairs of the Middle Ages, at which events of the year were passed in review in comic song and spectacle."[2] The notion of lighthearted musical commentary on the events of the day has continued to be the single most common feature of shows known as revues. Wolcott Gibbs called the revue "a cornucopia, a grab bag, a hash."[3] The great English producer Charles B. Cochran described the revue as:

> This most difficult form of theatrical entertainment.... It can combine the topical realism of an evening paper with the aloof symbolism of abstract ballet.... It can lame you with reasons or convulse you with irrational mirth. It can vary from intimacy, simplicity of scene, to grandiose spectacle, or from the broad clowning of the circus ring to the scintillating foil-play of the intellectual *escrime*.[4]

However he may have chosen to describe it, Rose felt that he could assemble a highly palatable theatrical hash. After all, he had Fanny Brice and the services of several clever writers to start with. All he really needed was a major investor, someone with some reputation and experience to help get the project started.

Among the various show business figures that passed in and out of Brice's circle was a young producer named Jed Harris. Harris, who in his twenties had become the boy wonder of Broadway, was fascinated with Brice and utterly perplexed by her marriage to Rose. For his part, Rose was fascinated with

Harris, who represented the sophisticated and literary world of the legitimate stage, a part of the theatre Rose had never encountered. Determined to win Harris's respect, Rose immersed himself in Shakespeare, Ibsen, Chekhov and Shaw, much in the manner of his plunge into songwriting. While he may never have become well versed in the great playwrights, Rose did succeed in convincing Harris to put up $10,000 for the revue he wanted to produce. Despite the urging of several friends that he change the title, Rose insisted on calling the show *Corned Beef and Roses*.[5]

In 1930 Rose began assembling, largely at Harris's suggestion, a first-rate production team. Alexander Leftwich staged the production, Jo Mielziner designed the sets, and Busby Berkeley and Danny Dare choreographed the dance sequences. David Freedman wrote most of the sketches, with Don Marquis, Ring Lardner and Peter Arno providing additional material. The music, which was listed glibly in the program as "by Mr. Rose and His Friends," included such eventual hits as "Would You Like to Take a Walk?" by Rose, Mort Dixon and Harry Warren, and "Cheerful Little Earful," which Ira Gershwin and Harry Warren wrote (with some assistance from Rose). Demonstrating the instincts of a true producer, Rose had comely Hannah Williams sing "Earful" and play the ingénue. Williams was engaged to the son of powerful New York banker Otto Kahn, who subsequently provided much of the show's long-term backing. In addition to Brice, the revue featured George Jessel and Hal Skelly, the dance team of Moss and Fontana, and the young Arthur Treacher.

Corned Beef and Roses was a hodgepodge of acts strung together with little regard for continuity. It failed to achieve the well-honed satiric and topical flavor of the various annual revues then in vogue, and while it sought to accommodate the specialties of its three stars, little effort was wasted on fitting the various parts together. *Corned Beef and Roses* had neither the lavish opulence of a Ziegfeld show nor the chic naughtiness of an Earl Carroll revue. The show's smorgasbord nature was an insurance policy against complete failure. It was also an extension of Rose's theory of song writing: if you cranked out enough material, some of it was bound to catch on.

Although Rose initially envisioned the show as an "intimate revue," with a minimum of elaborate settings, costumes and big chorus numbers, he ended up with something else entirely. Having booked the show into the Shubert Theatre in Philadelphia, Rose arrived the week before dress rehearsals to find the theatre's alley filled with scenery. Asking when the other production was going to be removed, he was told that the trappings belonged to his show. "Mielziner showed me little sketches," he exclaimed. "I thought the scenes would be little." Staring up at one particularly formidable-looking set piece, he remarked, "I never knew a lampost could be forty feet high!"[6]

Mielziner's own notes and designs for the show give little indication of an intimate or small-scale production. There are towering drops, a lavishly painted raked revolve and flats with as many as a dozen working doors. He prepared detailed drawings for over twenty scenes, each with its own set pieces, drops and groundrows. One chorus number featured a skyscraper platform designed to telescope to a height of over forty feet while chorines danced around its base. While not all of these fanciful creations made it to opening night, enough survived to clog the rear entrance of the Shubert.[7]

There were other problems as well. Shortly before the scheduled opening in Philadelphia, George Jessel went public with a dispute over his lines. It seemed that the opening sketch of the first act, written by Peter Arno, began with the line, "You lousy bastard!" After a week's delay and the rescheduling of opening night to October 14, Jessel and Rose finally reached an accommodation. "I have been given permission to delete anything in my role that I consider indecent," Jessel told the press. "Some of these lines have been said on the stage in the past, but that does not alter my opinion of them."[8]

By the time the show reached the boards, it had generated a considerable amount of curiosity. Jessel's public tussle over the wholesomeness of his dialogue and the prurient speculation fanned by Rose's press agents, had led stolid Philadelphia to expect the worst. *Variety*'s review confirmed the rumors: "In fact, it is generally agreed in Philly that *Corned Beef and Roses* is the dirtiest show ever witnessed here.... This [one of Jessel's routines] wasn't just off-color; it was lower-class stag-smoker stuff, and many a blasé theatregoer was hard put to keep from blushing. Even Jessel was embarrassed."[9]

The show opened with a lampoon of producers entitled "Poor Mr. Shufeld," in which Jessel played a harried composite of several well-known impresarios. Although the subject matter was rather shopworn, Jessel managed to make the time-honored couch scene in the producer's office play one more time, as *Variety* noted:

> Plenty of smut, but generally funny, with the chorus coming in in decorous black gowns, and then disrobing to demonstrate flashing pink undies, in which they do a wiggle dance in a big way. Jessel complains of a lame back and adds that he has been up all night working on the play. Blackout uses a suddenly appearing divan with a sign over it, "Casting tonight."[10]

After this, Brice, Skelly and Jessel entered together for the first time. On the drop behind them were posters and scenes from their respective Hollywood films, providing each with an opportunity to poke fun at themselves on screen. Their refrain informed the audience that they were back on stage, "at the request of Mr. Zukor, Mr. Warner and Mr. Fox."[11]

Jessel's first song of the evening was "When Pansy Was a Flower," a bit of musical social commentary all too obviously revealed by its title. He was followed by the only genuinely well-received musical number of the evening, Hannah Williams's rendition of "Cheerful Little Earful." Williams's coy but fresh presentation of Ira Gershwin's lyric gave the show a much needed lift.

The first act finale, "Stocks and Blondes," presented an elaborate setting of the New York Stock Exchange, but failed to get off the ground, despite two huge stock tickers that spewed tape while confetti rained down on the set.

The second act opened with "Angel Ballet," an inventive sequence of dance and tableaux conceived by Tamara Geva. While it involved little more than a dozen or so marginally clad ladies moving and posing behind a gossamer scrim, it was perceived as one of the show's more "tasteful and artistic" sequences.[12]

Although, according to *Variety*, the second act "plumbed the depths," Brice and Jessel had a few passable routines. Brice performed a droll and appropriate song parody by Rose and Lou Alter titled "I Wonder Who's Keeping Him Now" and a Rudolph Valentino send-up, "I Knew Him before He Was Spanish." Jessel then appeared as a Hungarian professor giving a stereopticon slide lecture described both as "a highly amusing, if considerably less than immaculate interlude," and "the dirtiest bit in the show."[13]

After a disastrous week in Philadelphia, Rose delayed the New York opening to buy time for an overhaul. Despite the advice of his associates, including Brice, that he close the show and cut his losses, Rose refused. He remained convinced that sharpening the dialogue and trimming the excessive scenery would save the production.

Dialogue and sets were not the only elements due for a change. A week after the press branded *Corned Beef and Roses* a failure, Hal Skelly left the cast. Apparently agreeing with the reviewers that he had "very little to do," Skelly gave notice and took another engagement. Rose lured James Barton, the popular dancer and comedian, away from the Shuberts' *Artists and Models* to take Skelly's place.[14] New specialty acts were also added, including "Borrah Minevitch and His Musical Rascals," an uproarious act that featured arrangements of classical and popular standards by an orchestra of sixty harmonicas, ocarinas and jew's harps.

With Barton in the cast less than three weeks, the show opened at the 46th Street Theatre on November 17 under the new title *Sweet and Low*. Freedman and others had finally convinced Rose that the original title "sounded like amateur night in the Bronx."[15] Although still in a state of more or less constant revision, things had improved noticeably since Philadelphia. The Manhattan reviewers were quick to note that, although the show might seem audacious to some, there was little in the way of novelty. "Those who attend the Palace... will find that not all of the material... is new," wrote the *New York Times*. "But most of the old stuff is sufficiently dressed up to make a repetition bearable."[16]

Much of the added flair seems to have come from Barton, who did turns as a Chinese and as an Irish drunk in addition to his renowned dance routines (fig. 2). Brice and Jessel also benefited from new material and the elimination of several of the less successful sequences. Brice did a few torch songs in Bronx and cockney dialects, as well as "Babykins," a precursor of her famous Baby Snooks routine. In this version, Arthur Treacher attempted to placate the outsized infant (fig. 3).

Although business was slow at first, Rose promoted the show to the hilt. From an average weekly gross of less than $30,000 in November, the show was earning nearly $60,000 a week by mid-January. Much of the turnaround was probably attributable to the generally held notion that the show was dirty. Although Rose did his best to perpetuate the idea, the dailies were the main source of *Sweet and Low*'s reputation. Alison Smith of the *New York World* decried the revue as containing "the sort of jokes that used to result in muffled guffaws behind the livery stable.... Now we know what becomes of unpleasant little boys who scrawl with chalk on fences. They grow up to write revues like *Sweet and Low*."[17]

Rose certainly relished the interest that such journalistic indignation generated, but in fact his show was not nearly as shameless as some made it out to be. *Sweet and Low*'s reputation for naughty dialogue was greatly overstated. Most of its gags were fairly tame, as the following samples indicate:

Williams: He wears such snappy clothes.
Barton: They should be snappy. He buys them with rubber checks.

Williams: Take me for a drive.
Barton: Can't. Tire's punctured.
Williams: How did that happen?
Barton: I ran over a bottle.
Williams: Why couldn't you miss it?
Barton: I couldn't see it. A guy had it in his pocket.

Brice: Last night I dreamt that the animal this fur came from was going to claw me to pieces.
Jessel: Don't tell me you're afraid of a rabbit.[18]

Although *Sweet and Low* did achieve a certain degree of popularity, it had barely managed to break even when Rose closed the show in April.[19] Although he briefly toyed with the idea of a summer version entitled *Sweeter and Lower,* better judgment somehow prevailed. The following month Rose unveiled a revamped version of *Sweet and Low* called *Crazy Quilt*. Brice was still in the cast, but Phil Baker and Ted Healy replaced Barton and Jessel. There were a few other new wrinkles, including one of Rose's classic songs, "I Found a Million Dollar Baby in a Five and Ten Cent Store."[20]

For the most part, however, *Crazy Quilt* was not much more than *Sweet and Low* retitled, with a few new songs and performers thrown in. The show's survival depended almost entirely on vigorous promotion and the sort of

Figure 2. Arthur Treacher and Fanny Brice in *Sweet and Low*, 1930
(Courtesy Billy Rose Theatre Collection, New York Public Library, Astor, Lenox and Tilden Foundations)

Figure 3. James Barton and Fanny Brice in *Sweet and Low*, 1930
(Courtesy Billy Rose Theatre Collection, New York Public Library, Astor, Lenox and Tilden Foundations)

unabashed public hustle that was becoming Rose's trademark as a producer. Those who claim that Billy Rose was not born but merely created by press agents are not far from the truth. Rose cultivated the Broadway columnists and convinced many of them, especially Walter Winchell and Lucius Beebe, that he was a genuinely interesting and eccentric character whose exploits would make amusing copy.

Beginning with *Crazy Quilt,* it becomes difficult to separate Rose and Rose's productions from the hype surrounding them. Through the offices of Richard Maney, Charles Washburne and other press agents, the papers regularly mentioned Rose's name, his shows, his plans and his peccadilloes. He firmly believed, as Barnum had once said, that you did not read publicity, you measured it. Rose did not care what was printed about him as long as his name and the address of the theatre were correct. His debt to Barnum's style of hard sell is evident in the advertisements he ran during *Crazy Quilt:*

> The theatre is the only business—if it is a business—that hasn't recognized the current depression by reducing prices. I am not moved by charitable reasons but by sound economic sense when I charge from $.50 to $4.40 for what, by normal standards, is a $6.60 revue. I want to play to a full house and I don't think a house can be filled for $6.60.
> —Billy Rose[21]

In spite of price reductions and aggressive advertisements, *Crazy Quilt* never really caught on. Still, Rose refused to write the production off. He spent $150,000 before the show began to turn a profit. Where other producers would have closed out and cut their losses, Rose kept plugging away, as if rejection of his show was a rejection of him. In a way it was; he tied himself so closely to his shows that they became extensions of his personality. Some producers tried to guess what people wanted; Billy Rose prescribed to them. Biographer Earl Conrad called this talent "a gift for reviving dead horses... and making the public like it and pay for it, as if he knew best what was good for them."[22]

Despite Rose's prodigious infusions of money and energy, *Crazy Quilt* lasted barely two months. This time he was unable to recover all of his or anyone else's investment: *Crazy Quilt*'s red ink added up to nearly $100,000. The day after the show closed, a press agent named Ned Alvord walked into Rose's office. Rose describes the encounter: "He was sporting a seersucker cutaway, a derby hat and a turned-around collar like a minister. In a train-whistle voice he announced I could get my dough back if I had the guts to juice up the show, take it to the hinterlands, and sell it like Barnum used to sell his circus."[23]

Alvord had earned the nickname "Deacon" for his somber clothes and foghorn voice. He also had a reputation for reviving failed shows and inducing rural audiences to flock to them. One of his favorite stunts was to appear in a small town a week or so in advance of the show he was promoting. He would go to the local newspaper just before press time and tell the print foreman that the wrong advertisement had been sent and a substitution was necessary. Before the editor or anyone at the paper could approve it, Alvord would slip in a panel depicting a bevy of bosomy, nearly nude girls surrounded by equally voluptuous prose which described the show. "A Saturnalia of Wanton Rhythm... 50 Hoydens Unwrapped for Hot Weather... Voluptuous Houris" and similar phrases promised a cavalcade of unclad delights. The following day, Alvord went, in his best clerical outfit, to the local ministers and told them that an unbelievably wicked entertainment was about to descend on their town. The men of the cloth denounced the filthy show from their pulpits, and the public turned out in droves to see Alvord's evil production.[24]

Alvord's promised resuscitation of *Crazy Quilt* prompted Rose to consider a major reworking of the entire production. Herman Rosse, who had designed the sets for *Crazy Quilt,* was on his way to Rose's office to discuss plans for the touring production when he ran into an old friend, John Murray Anderson. Anderson, who had just finished staging the new Shubert show *Life Begins at 8:40,* had a considerable reputation as a director whose elegant style had made a success of such revues as the *Greenwich Village Follies.* Never having met Rose, Anderson asked Rosse if he could accompany him to the meeting. As Anderson later noted, it was, "a propitious meeting for us both. Just as Picasso passed through a 'Periode de la Rosse,' I was about to enter... the 'Rose Period' of my career." Rose told him of his plan to send *Crazy Quilt* on tour. Anderson replied that he was "familiar with that kind of show, was at the moment unemployed, and could I stage it for him." Rose quickly agreed, and an agreement was signed that day.[25]

Crazy Quilt played the East and Midwest for nearly a year. The promotional prose was ripe, even for Alvord:

El Bolero!—
 Torrid as the Passion Laden Zephyrs From Its Native Andalusia!

The Loveliest of Womankind!—
 Three Score Delectable Buds plucked from the ROSE GARDENS of Broadway. A Bazaar of Comeliness such as only the Master Connoisseur of Feminine Charm BILLY ROSE could conceive and place upon a single stage![26]

Anderson's revived version played to packed houses. The mayor of Minneapolis banned it. Local reviewers were scandalized. Rose's mix of vaudeville, burlesque and a few well-known entertainers caught the fancy of the rural public. Anderson was one of the first to see the fruits of Rose's flop turned moneymaker. The day before the show opened in Cleveland, Rose doubled the amount specified in Anderson's contract.[27]

After wringing every dollar he could from Alvord's fiercely promoted tour of *Crazy Quilt*, Rose turned to a different project. During the runs of *Sweet and Low* and *Crazy Quilt*, he had struck up a friendship with Ben Hecht, one of Broadway's more successful commercial writers. In the spring of 1932 Hecht brought Rose a script coauthored with Gene Fowler, originally entitled *Carousel* and finally called *The Great Magoo*. The play was yet another variation on the backstage romance theme, one whose glib preciosity is best captured by the authors' own description of it on the title page of the original typescript: "A Love Sick Charade in 3 Acts and something like nine scenes recounting the didoes of two young and amorous souls who nigh perished when they weren't in the hay together.... This simple and slightly uncouth saga is the work of Messrs. Ben Hecht and Gene Fowler."[28]

Despite the work's limited potential, Rose went for it with little persuasion. "I doubt he ever really read the thing," recounts Richard Maney. "Even if he did he wouldn't have known if it was any good or not. Plays just weren't his strong suit."[29] Aside from his interest in the script, Rose wanted to impress Hecht and Fowler. As with his earlier efforts to impress Jed Harris, Rose was fascinated with genuine talent and wanted to be as close to it as possible. "It wasn't always cynical," said Maney. "He really wanted those people to like him, to approve of him."[30]

Rose needed talent around him almost as much as publicity or power. He sought the energy and ideas of people like Hecht and Fowler as catalysts to his own thoughts. Rose could be quite creative, provided somebody else had the initial inspiration. As with *Sweet and Low* and *Crazy Quilt*, he spared no expense in obtaining top-notch personnel. He enlisted George Abbott to direct and Herman Rosse to design the settings, which included some striking scenes of Coney Island's midway and boardwalk. The show opened at the Selwyn Theatre on December 2, 1932 to reviews that were hardly charitable. Brooks Atkinson compared it to "a tabloid serial... all rather stale and malodorous."[31] Robert Garland of the *New York World Telegram* wrote that Hecht and Fowler reminded him "of a pair of precocious boys showing off before company, plotting and planning just how far they will be allowed to go."[32] In this instance, they were allowed one week. *The Great Magoo* closed, and Rose found himself out nearly $75,000.

One of the few things to survive from the show was its only song, "If You Believe in Me," a bouncy tune written by Harold Arlen with words by Rose and E. Y. Harburg. The following year it was retitled and became one of the biggest hits of the decade. If any one song summed up the way Billy Rose saw himself and his world, this was it:

22 *"Broadway Billy"*

> Say it's only a paper moon
> Sailing over a cardboard sea
> But it wouldn't be make believe
> If you believed in me....
> It's a Barnum and Bailey world
> Just as phony as it can be
> But it wouldn't be make believe
> If you believed in me.[33]

Not long after *The Great Magoo* closed, Max Arronsen paid Rose another visit. A group of mobsters had rented the Gallo Theatre (formerly the New Yorker) on Fifty-fourth Street west of Broadway. They had no idea of what to do with it and wanted Rose to run the place. Although he had no desire for another partnership with what he half-jokingly referred to as "the Rod and Gun Club," the idea of having a theatre of his own intrigued him. Rose negotiated a contract under which he would be paid $1000 a week to produce shows for the theatre. The contract also stipulated that Rose's name was to appear prominently in all advertisements and programs. The productions were to remain Rose's property, and he was to be given absolute control of their content. He also insisted that $100,000 be provided up front to remodel the theatre. The mob agreed, and Rose went to work.[34]

He had a notion that he could combine successful elements from his earlier shows into a single production. It had to have music, comedy and the sort of heightened side-show flavor of *Crazy Quilt*. To keep up interest and insure a tidy profit, there needed to be liquor and food for sale. Above all, the thing had to command attention. Being simply interesting or diverting was not enough; this project had to be a sensation. The idea of a cabaret seemed perfect, but not a conventional cabaret. With a building the size of the New Yorker, an entirely different approach was required. Rose's concept was simple. "Vaudeville came from the beer hall," he observed. "They separated refreshments from vaudeville and what happened? Vaudeville died. A floor show is an effort to bring a little of the theatre into a restaurant. So when repeal came I said:—'Why not put a whole restaurant into a theatre?'"[35]

He wasted little time. To start with, Rose removed the theatre's seats, terraced the house, and put in tables and chairs. He then began a crash course on the history of New York cabaret entertainment. Once again, Rose was doing his homework. He talked to a number of former cabaret and nightclub owners to get a general idea of how to approach the project: "The man whose plans most nearly paralleled my own was Jesse Lasky, who tried to convert the Fulton Theatre into a casino about twenty years ago and lost $800,000 in twenty-eight weeks. We took him as a model and did the exact opposite in every detail."[36]

Lasky's club had a five-dollar cover charge, so Rose had none. Lasky had required formal evening dress; Rose left the question of attire open. Instead of orchestras playing waltzes and gavottes, Rose had Benny Goodman and other popular jazz musicians.

When Casino de Paree opened its doors on December 15, 1933, Rose did not just settle for a single orchestra; there were two bands playing in rotation so that customers enjoyed continuous music. In addition to orchestras, stage shows, newsreels, singing waiters and novelty acts, Rose allowed patrons to dance on-stage during those few moments when nothing else was going on. For those too inhibited to dance before a crowd, there was a cellophane curtain at midstage to conceal the features of shy customers.[37]

A card was placed on each table for the benefit of those ladies whose male companions might not be too light of feet. Following a reproduction of the opening lyrics of "Just a Gigolo," the card read:

TO THE LADIES:
May I present a group of sophisticated, amazingly handsome young men? If Madame's escort doesn't feel like dancing, she can 'trip the light fantastic' with Mr. Three or Mr. Seven. (They have no names.) They see, they hear, but remember nothing! You'll know them by their lapels. LOOK FOR THE GREEN CARNATION! Upon a request to the waiter, one of these gentlemen will come to your table.
BILLY ROSE[38]

Beyond watching their fellow patrons and the gigolos, the audience was treated to a variety of entertainments that were, to say the least, eclectic. Unlike its notable precursors, such as Ziegfeld's Roof Garden, Rose's cabaret did not aspire to sophistication. In addition to such conventional cabaret types as tap dancer Eleanor Powell and torch singer Gertrude Niesen, Rose engaged a number of eccentric specialty acts. There was Chaz Chase, a comedian billed as "The Man Who Will Eat You Out of House and Home." Chase indeed possessed a voracious and somewhat indiscriminate appetite. He ate his lighted cigar, the flower in his buttonhole, his cufflinks and the collar of his dress shirt. To top things off, he took several bites of his violin.[39]

Also on hand was Eddie Eddy, the cry artist, whose real tears poured into the footlights several times each evening. There was a clown with electric eyes who hypnotized patrons, and a man who sat on a pyramid of milk bottles held aloft by Tyana the Strong Woman. The fire-eating Magfys performed while Andy Kennedy played jazz favorites on the spoons. The Fat Girl Ballet (now without competition from the Shuberts) also appeared, and there was a nudist bar downstairs where patrons observed naked women in gigantic fishbowls. Strolling gypsies took photographs of the guests, read palms and sold tobacco.

"Broadway Billy"

The carnivallike chaos of the place continued nonstop from 6:00 P.M. to 2:00 A.M. *New York Herald Tribune* columnist Lucius Beebe described the club as combining "the more delirious features of the Winter Garden, the Hall of Mirrors at Versailles, a Durbar at Delhi, and the cafe of the Griswold Hotel at New London on boat race night.... There were maidens unrobing in mirrored devices and professors performing upon stringed instruments.... Halloween at the madhouse was never like this."[40]

This incredible assemblage of acts did not come together by accident. When he first got the idea for using variety entertainers, Rose sent a seasoned vaudeville agent named Jack Lewis to scour the country. For months Lewis prowled small-time theatres from coast to coast and sent potential acts to New York for Rose's review. Rose told Beebe, "I guess I've had fifty auditions altogether and have seen more than 5,000 short acts. I wanted troupers who... had that O. Henry boarding house look."[41]

In addition to providing these performers with a chance to be seen in New York, Rose and Hecht wrote a routine for them called the "Small Time Cavalcade." Before the small timers appeared, a master of ceremonies came out to give them a musical introduction:

> Allow me friends to introduce,
> Professor, if you please,
> The artists of the vaudeville stage,
> That Broadway never sees.
> Masters of the laugh and tear,
> Clowns and Jesters gay,
> Playing the tank towns year on year
> And dreaming of Broadway.
> Give them that big hand of yours,
> This is their big time shot,
> Behold the cornbelt troubadours,
> The acts that Keith forgot:
>
> *(small timers sing)*
>
> For 20 years we played the sticks
> For coffee and for cakes
> For 20 years we played the sticks
> And never got the breaks
> In stuffy Pullman uppers
> We have traveled everywheres
> And snatched our midnight suppers
> Off of greazy one-arm chairs.
> Upon a 1000 stages, we have made them laugh and cry,
> But *Variety* won't notice us until the day we die.
>
> *(patter)*

> In Wichita, in Chickasaw, in Haverstraw and Niles,
> In Kankakee and Laramee, we laid 'em in the aisles.
> In Pontiac, in Fondulac, in Hackensack and Flint,
> In spots that even Rand McNally never cared to print.
> In rooming houses, boarding houses, broken down hotels,
> Playing four a day and five a day, we went through
>   fifty hells.
> Our object and our aim,
> The chance that never came.[42]

Rose produced other equally memorable musical numbers for Casino de Paree including "Uncle Tom's Cabin is a Roadhouse Now" and the genuinely charming song, "Have a Little Dream on Me."[43]

The entire agglomeration proved immensely popular. Casino de Paree was soon grossing more than $40,000 a week, and the press was raving (fig. 4). Even the normally reserved George Jean Nathan seemed impressed: "If this Billy Rose thing spreads," he wrote, "it probably won't be long before Katherine Cornell will be doing her acting to the accompaniment of banged beer seidels and the Theatre Guild will be booking some of its productions at Luchows's or the Waldorf Astoria Roof Garden."[44]

The overflow crowds at Casino de Paree convinced Rose's underworld bosses to back his plans for a second club in the Hammerstein Theatre around the corner from Casino de Paree at Broadway and Fifty-third Street. Christened the Billy Rose Music Hall, the new establishment was patterned after Casino de Paree, only more so. Female dance partners were added in the manner of the numbered gigolos at Casino de Paree. There was a Gay Nineties–style bar downstairs called the Barbary Coast, where the floor was paved with silver dollars and the waitresses often wore little more than a garter and a smile. The bar also featured a wishing well that offered glimpses of nude maidens via mirrors inside the well. People still danced on-stage, only this time a sky cyclorama filled with stars and live birch trees in the wings gave patrons the sensation of dancing outdoors on a summer night. The new theatre opened on June 21, 1934, with prices and publicity even more eye-catching than for Casino de Paree (fig. 5).

From Rose's point of view, the best part of the new place was the sign on the roof, a huge electric billboard forty feet high that spelled out "BILLY ROSE." "The first night it was burning," Rose recalls, "I went outside to admire it. As I stood on the corner, I heard someone ask, 'Billy Rose, who's that?' 'That's Fanny Brice's husband,' someone answered."[45]

Obviously the songs, the revues, the nightclubs—none of it had been enough. Even forty feet worth of blinking lights on Broadway had not done the trick. It was then that Billy Rose resolved to concoct something so spectacular that people would be talking about Mrs. Rose and not Mr. Brice.

WHAT IS IT?

IS IT A THEATRE ... NO!!
though on a STAGE we present a full length musical extravaganza produced by **BILLY ROSE**.

IS IT A RESTAURANT . NO!!
though you eat and drink what you will (thanks to Liquor License No. RL-733).

IS IT A DANCE HALL . NO!!
though there is continuous dancing to the music of two of America's great orchestras.

IS IT A SIDE SHOW .. NO!!
though in an ordinary size FISH BOWL you see a completely nude LIVING little lady.

WHAT IS IT?

It's the Most Sensational Bargain in the history of New York Night Life!!!

BELIEVE IT OR NOT! FOR $2
you get the Revue, the Dinner, the Dancing, The Girl in the Fish Bowl, and a hundred other novelties—

Casino de Paree

54th Street
West of Broadway

Opens at 6 P.M.
Tel. Cir. 7-2686

What the Critics Say—

WALTER WINCHELL in the *Daily Mirror* ...
"New York has a smash—not for just a night, not for just a year—but ALL WAYS"

PERCY HAMMOND in the *Herald-Tribune* ...
"In a care-free, *luxurious*, and *inexpensive* atmosphere, a spectacular stage show performed by a bevy of fifty of Times Square's most ornamental lady exhibitionists designed to gratify the greediest investigator of female shape celestial."

ED SULLIVAN in the *Daily News* ...
"The best musical show in New York."

ROBERT GARLAND in the *World-Telegram* ...
"If you ask me, I like the Casino de Paree. With a show you enjoy, air to breathe, a stage to dance on, and excellent service, it is *a solution to your after midnight problem.*"

BERNARD SOBEL in the *Daily Mirror* ..
"*Paris is right around the corner now*—the Casino de Paree, gilded, gala, gay! If you have any doubt about this happy circumstance, rush right over and see the show. You will be captivated. You will say to yourself: 'After longing for Paris all my life, I have it here,—a music hall with all the abandon and flare of the Follies Bergere.'"

ABEL in *Variety* ...
"It has all the ear-marks of becoming a New York landmark. Comparable to the former Ziegfeld Roof; Follies Bergere; Casino de Paree; Les Ambassadeurs, and Moulin Rouge of Paris; Kit Kat of London; or the Cassinova of Berlin. Truly the most unusual cafe in the world, *combining* as it does the *better features* of the American *theatre* with an after *supper club*."

WHITNEY BOLTON in the *Telegraph* .
"For my money, it's the best dining, dancing spot in town. *A show that's really beautiful to behold.* The crowd took the show with heavy applause and asked for more."

GEORGE ROSS in the *World-Telegram* .
"An array of talent as impressive as the Palace in its hey-day! A show as extravagant, as daring and as spectacular as anything you will find in a Roxy Hippodrome; in a Carroll Vanity; or in any of the Ziegfeldian Lady Godiva Settings."

Figure 4. Flyer for Casino de Paree
(Collection of the author)

Figure 5. Flyer for the Billy Rose Music Hall
(Collection of the author)

With his two theatres in full swing, Rose decided to take a trip to Europe, where he had heard that fabulous full-scale circuses still toured. Before closing his office for the trip, he sent a note to Brice, who was appearing in the Ziegfeld Follies at the Winter Garden. "Jean," he called to his secretary, "take a letter for Mrs. Billy Rose at the Winter Garden. If it gets delivered, I'll know I'm a success."[46] The note never arrived.

3

Jumbo

Rose returned from Europe to find some unwanted changes at Casino de Paree and the Billy Rose Music Hall. In less than two months, his underworld associates had practically bankrupted both clubs. Prices had been raised and the food and service were now abysmal. Many of the top acts were gone as well; Benny Goodman and Eleanor Powell had both been fired for no apparent reason. Several entertainers claimed to have been beaten up by mobsters when they tried to join the union. Nightclubs that only recently turned customers away were now losing money. In addition, the gangsters had neglected to pay Rose's salary during his eight weeks overseas, a total of $16,000.

When Rose complained about conditions at the nightclubs and the mob's failure to pay him according to the contract, he learned that the agreement meant little. "I wouldn't depend on that contract if I were you," one of them told him. "While you were in Europe, we shot out most of the clauses."[1] Rose told Walter Winchell about his confrontation with the mobsters. Winchell told him to be careful.

Rose was unperturbed. He loaded the scenery and costumes from both theatres into trucks and moved them to a warehouse in New Jersey. He then contacted Bernard Baruch. Baruch called Attorney General Homer Cummings, who in turn phoned J. Edgar Hoover. The next day, several G-men arrived at Rose's office. He gave them the names of the gangsters who had been involved with the clubs. The agents informed the mob that they were personally responsible for Rose's safety. Any harm to him would bring the wrath of the law down on all their operations.[2]

Despite the government's assurances that he would be protected, Rose took no chances. He ate most of his meals at home and employed several bodyguards when he and Fanny were out late. The mob, however, took the warning to heart. Rose withdrew from both clubs, made no attempt to recover his salary, and severed all ties with the underworld.[3] Within a few months, both nightclubs went out of business.

Following his successful confrontation with the mob, Rose's ego grew to even greater proportions. At times he actually seemed to believe the publicity that Richard Maney and Ned Alvord generated for him. The two press agents crafted an image of Rose as the "Bantum Barnum," an improbable mix of P. T. Barnum, Cecil B. De Mille and Florenz Ziegfeld. They cast him as a messiah of mass amusement whose every triumph would be more magnificent and astounding than the last. Rose believed this puffery and was determined to live up to it. Although he was, for the moment, unemployed, Rose was hardly out of circulation. His wife's lavish parties provided the ideal climate in which to cultivate a suitably grandiose project.

Among those on the Brice and Rose cocktail circuit was John Jay Whitney, who, with his sister Joan Payson, was heir to the enormous Whitney fortune. Rose had met Whitney through Herbert Bayard Swope, who was Bernard Baruch's vice-chairman at the War Industries Board. "Jock" Whitney (as he was called because of his polo exploits) was hardly the first socially prominent New Yorker to enjoy the company of show business people. He was, however, one of the few to be genuinely intrigued with Billy Rose.

Whitney enjoyed Rose's quick wit and contagious enthusiasm, but what really impressed him was Rose's knack of developing an idea, promoting it, managing it and making money with it. Rose had, after all, convinced the city's toughest gangsters to pour money into two losing theatres, which he then made the sensations of New York. He had also taken a revue written off for dead in Philadelphia and made it play for two seasons. Rose was well aware of Whitney's high opinion of him, and he carefully cultivated the young millionaire. He was also beginning to develop an idea for a new show. Although it was still a vague and unformed notion, Rose knew that it would require support commensurate with Whitney's resources.

In Europe Rose had seen two famous French indoor circuses, the Cirque Medrano and the Cirque d'Hiver. While staying at Baruch's hunting lodge in Czechoslovakia, he had also made a side trip to Budapest to see a play about a circus. It was a romantic musical staged outdoors, with clowns and jugglers added for atmosphere.[4] The show reminded Rose of the "Small Time Cavalcade" he and Hecht had written for Casino de Paree. It occurred to him that the circus provided an ideal format for the type of entertainment he wanted to produce. If a restaurant and a nightclub could be put into a theatre, then why not a circus?

"I felt I needed a big medium to channel all my energies," he later recalled. "The super-spectacle, the Big Show appealed to me. I knew the life stories of Barnum, of Thompson and Dundy, of the Ringling brothers. I knew that all who had functioned in the spectacle field were dead. If I was looking for a field devoid of competition... that required a certain kind of desperado cockeyed showmanship,... this was it."[5]

Rose knew that circuses were no longer a unique or wildly popular form of entertainment. "Strong children drag weak parents to the circus," he told Maney. "But do any adults in their right mind attend the circus in successive years? Find me one and I'll have him hauled before a lunacy commission."[6] What Rose had in mind involved combining the more exciting and spectacular elements of the circus with the showgirl side of the Broadway musical. "Men may sicken at the sight of an elephant on its hind legs," he observed, "but consider the state of their pulse when they are permitted to gaze on 1,000 beautiful young women."[7]

The show would incorporate everything Rose thought the public liked: thrills, music, action, girls and spectacle, all on a scale beyond even the most elaborate Broadway extravaganza. He had originally thought of taking the show on the road in tents, but soon realized a Broadway production was the only way to distinguish his endeavor from an overblown carnival. It was also the only way to rid himself of the sobriquet "Mr. Fanny Brice." The main obstacles were money and a theatre that could house such a gargantuan spectacle.

Rose assumed that Whitney would provide the financing if shown a tantalizing sample of the finished product. He promptly commissioned Ben Hecht and Charles MacArthur to write the script and Rodgers and Hart to compose the music and lyrics. Hecht had been in a circus briefly as a youth and loved the idea. MacArthur suggested that the show be called *Jumbo*, after Barnum's famous elephant. Within a few weeks Hecht and MacArthur had fleshed out the basic plot. It was a neatly contrived tale of two rival circus owners whose son and daughter fall in love and ultimately save the day for all concerned. MacArthur's tongue-in-cheek plot description indicates that neither writer took the work too seriously: "It's about an Irish circus owner who likes to hit the bottle, and it's his habit to let his elephant go on a spree with him," MacArthur told a colleague. "On the boss's birthday they both get drunk and the elephant sees pink men."[8]

While his writers may have been a trifle glib, Rose was completely in earnest. He engaged George Abbott to direct the interludes of dialogue and John Murray Anderson to stage the production's dances and circus sequences. Raoul Pène duBois would design the costumes and Albert Johnson the settings.[9] Rose began hiring this array of Broadway talent before he had found either a theatre or substantial backing. For three months, while his production team toiled over scripts, designs and scores, Rose engaged performers and secured rehearsal spaces. He rented the abandoned Union Church on Forty-eighth Street and the stage of the Manhattan Opera House. Rose also leased several acres at Teevan's Riding Academy in Brooklyn and began collecting animals. To aid him in his search, he hired Allan Foster, who had some equestrian experience and had been dance director at the Winter Garden.

Foster was also supposed to stage the riding events once the horses were found. This proved to be no easy task, and after two weeks the only animal in the *Jumbo* menagerie was a goat Foster had bought in Connecticut for $2.50. Part of the problem was Anderson's insistence that the horses be only pure white Arabians and jet black stallions. "We'd have had the horses two weeks ago if it hadn't been for Murray Anderson," Rose noted. "He wants them all to have eyes like Lola Montez."[10]

Foster dispensed several circus trainers to Kentucky and Tennessee to search for horses. Rose meanwhile put out the call for acts and assorted animals. A number of the vaudeville performers from Casino de Paree and the Billy Rose Music Hall were engaged, and various circus acts were auditioned. The man who sold Foster the goat turned out to be the proprietor of an act called "Snyder's Comedy Goat and Monkey Circus." When one of Snyder's monkeys lit Rose's cigarette while standing on a goat, Rose hired the act on the spot.

Once word circulated that Rose needed circus acts and animals, he was besieged with hundreds of suggestions. These included Mme. Camille's Blue Ribbon Pomeranians ("An Aggregation of Cost, Originality, Merit, and Beauty... a Continual Paradox") and a man from Elizabeth, New Jersey who "wondered if you could use any or both of the following: a six-legged pig or a six-legged lamb, both ALIVE." A gentleman named A. N. Tuyum claimed to have been "assigned by the Soviet Government the task of disposing of a great number of wild animals from Siberia and the Caucasas [*sic*]." Tuyum's rather curious sense of Russian climate and geography became evident when he described the available beasts. "These include leopards, tigers, lions, pumas, cheetahs, jaguars and other products of the wild forest country."[11]

Despite the considerable task of finding legitimate sources for exotic animals, Rose began to make headway. The elephant that would play Jumbo was rented from Coney Island's Luna Park. Although Barnum's pachyderm was a male, Rose assumed that only another elephant would notice that his own three-ton star was a female. He was particularly fond of her name: Big Rosie. The Benson Animal Farm of Nashua, New Hampshire agreed to lease Rose nearly 1200 animals for $1500 a week. Llamas and camels were rented. Storks, jaguars and wolves were added for novelty. Monkeys, donkeys, pigeons, tigers, reindeer, lions, bears, and all the assorted bestiary of the big top began to assemble at Teevan's. The smell and the noise began to get the attention of the neighbors. "Does Rose think there's going to be another flood, or what?" quipped one local resident.[12]

The next step was acquiring a suitable theatre. Rose discussed the problem with Bernard Baruch. Madison Square Garden was too big, and most of the other theatre owners balked at the radical interior modifications Rose wanted. He had failed to convince RKO, the owners of the immense

Hippodrome (located on Sixth Avenue at Fiftieth Street), to rent him what would have been the ideal theatre. Baruch, however, had inside information that the Hippodrome was about to be sold, and that its new owners intended to tear the structure down in less than a year and put up a huge office tower.[13]

The great theatre had proved unprofitable for years and was now the occasional home of vagrant opera companies, basketball games, political rallies and wrestling matches. The stage that once supported such lavish productions as Thompson and Dundy's *A Yankee Circus on Mars* had fallen into disrepair. Max Reinhardt had considered putting his *Eternal Road* into the Hippodrome, but changed his mind when he learned of the theatre's condition. The new owners decided that its life as a performance space was over and were preparing to develop the site for commercial use. Had Rose been discreet about his plans, he might have rented the hall for as little as $1000 a week. However, with stories already circulating about Rose's great indoor circus, the Hippodrome's proprietors held out for the best possible deal. In the end, they made $6000 a week at the peak of *Jumbo*'s run.[14]

Rose was not one to let such haggling interfere with his plans. While he negotiated with the theatre's owners, he secured their permission to begin using the Hippodrome for rehearsals. Rose immediately had designer Albert Johnson remove all the orchestra seats and build an immense circus ring that extended to the middle of the orchestra section (fig. 6). To give the feel of a big top, new seating raked downward from the balcony to the ring and surrounded it on three sides. Nearly two months before he had a legal right to modify the building, Rose had completely transformed the Hippodrome. For weeks the theatre was in absolute disarray, leading Rose to declare, "The place looks like the inside of Earl Carroll's stomach."[15]

Because the renovations exposed much of the Hippodrome's decaying interior, Johnson began a massive restoration of the entire building. Steam blasters scrubbed off years of grime from all of the theatre's exposed surfaces. The house was repainted in various shades of red, with a deep blue ceiling trimmed in white and gold to make it resemble an immense big top. The lobby was redone in scarlet, gold and white, with particular attention paid to the ornate elephant heads that topped the pilasters. Beneath the lobby, the Hippodrome's old animal cages were reconstructed as a small zoo for the amusement of patrons before the show and at intermissions. The highlight of this menagerie was a papier-maché mountain swarming with monkeys, each of which wore a tag inscribed with the name of a Broadway celebrity. Rose denied the rumor that the monkeys would be named after his friends. "I haven't *that* many friends," he said.[16]

The stage also received lavish attention. John Murray Anderson vetoed Rose's idea of covering the ring in sawdust because of its adverse effect on the costumes. As a result, an extra $2000 had to be spent to fill the arena with a

Figure 6. Circus Ring for *Jumbo*, New York Hippodrome, 1935
(Courtesy Billy Rose Theatre Collection, New York Public Library, Astor, Lenox and Tilden Foundations)

four-inch mat of nonadhesive cocoa. Sachets of sawdust were then placed throughout the house to give the obligatory circus aroma. Immediately behind the ring, a revolve of equal size carried setpieces and the necessary circus paraphernalia. Albert Johnson's efforts also included the construction of a circular grid and catwalk above the ring to hold lights, rigging and the occasional performer (fig. 7).

The show was still in its formative stages when Rose realized that permanent financing was imperative. He had already spent $35,000 of his own money and desperately needed at least $200,000 more to complete renovations to the theatre and open the show. Rose promptly arranged an audition for Jock Whitney and his sister at which the various members of the production staff offered samples of their work.[17]

A week later, Anderson, Hecht, Rodgers, Hart and the others gathered in Rose's office for the momentous audition. Albert Johnson had made elaborate models of the settings and the modifications to the Hippodrome.

Figure 7. Catwalk for *Jumbo*, New York Hippodrome, 1935
(Courtesy Billy Rose Theatre Collection, New York Public Library, Astor, Lenox and Tilden Foundations)

Raoul Pène duBois presented a series of full-color costume renderings and material samples. Rodgers and Hart played what little of the score was complete. Rose, Hecht, Abbott and Anderson outlined the plot and staging of the show. "It was my first experience of an audition for 'angels,'" Anderson later recalled. "The last note of music had scarcely been struck when the young man said he would underwrite the venture." Anderson believed that the quality of the presentation had much to do with its success. "Today auditions are the rule.... But I have never seen one so expertly... given as this first one, planned and presented by Billy Rose for *Jumbo*. Rose seemed to be possessed of unbounded courage, energy and enthusiasm."[18]

Jumbo had been saved, and Rose once more became the cocky impresario. His press agent Maney came up with the line, "*Jumbo* will make me or break Jock Whitney." Rose even began greeting Whitney with the salutation, "Hiya, sucker." After a few weeks of this, Whitney decided to cut him down to size. He hired a man roughly Rose's height to show up at an audition. When Rose asked him what his specialty was, the man replied, "I'm a midget." Rose never learned that Whitney had arranged the incident.[19]

Despite such foolishness, casting proceeded on schedule. Foster took out an ad in the *New York Herald Tribune* calling for "Six foot showgirls and chorus girls who can combine dancing with equestrianism." The show's specialty acts included six "iron-jawed" girls (who held on to trapezes with their teeth), a giant, a midget, a human frog, and a man who juggled billiard balls with a sack over his head. Rose was approached by one agent who offered him a girl who could tap dance on a horse. Rose was unimpressed and told the man, "Come back when you get a horse tap dancing on a girl."[20]

Major stars were also being hired. Paul Whiteman and his orchestra were booked for $6000 a week. Rose even tried, unsuccessfully, to get Babe Ruth to appear in the show. He signed an old circus hand named Poodles Hanneford to play the ringmaster. Poodles's daughter was also cast as a bareback rider. Donald Novis, the radio personality, was cast as the male lead. Gloria Grafton played the sweetheart whom Novis serenaded from a galloping horse. The biggest casting coup was the engagement of Jimmy Durante to play the role of Claudius B. Bowers, a circus press agent modeled after Alvord and Maney (fig. 8). Durante was paid $3000 a week for antics that included lying down on-stage while an elephant walked over him. "Anybody who thinks I'm overpaid should try that duet with the elephant nine times a week...the trouble with Billy Rose is that he can convince you to do anything."[21]

As rehearsals progressed, Rose ran into trouble with Actors' Equity, which was unsure just what sort of show *Jumbo* was. If it was a legitimate stage production, performers had to be paid for rehearsals, whereas no such provision existed for the circus. To further the show's case as an offshoot of the circus, Rose had a clause inserted in the performer contracts that read: "In addition to salary, all performers will receive, in New York and on tour, meals, lodging and transportation common and customary in the circus business."[22]

Despite the performer's hardships (Foster's equestriennes had worked for six weeks without pay), Equity finally agreed that, since most of *Jumbo*'s performers were either animals or circus professionals, the show should be considered a circus and not a musical.[23] This decision was one of the contributing factors that led to the formation of the American Guild of Variety Artists several years later.[24]

The rehearsals themselves were bizarre, often harrowing affairs. Much of the show's success depended on split-second timing between acts that did not work together until dress rehearsals began. In one number called "Diavolo," a male chorus of thirty-six roustabouts had to construct a large animal cage from various sections in precisely sixty-four measures of music. At the

Figure 8. Jimmy Durante in *Jumbo*, New York Hippodrome, 1935
(Courtesy Billy Rose Theatre Collection, New York Public Library, Astor, Lenox and Tilden Foundations)

conclusion of this, six lions were to rush into the completed cage. After a count of eight, a trapeze artist was to fall into the cage at the same instant as a total blackout.

The aerialist, a Dutchman named Vabanque, had no ear for music and invariably fell into the cage at the wrong moment, thus spoiling the effect of the blackout. Finally, as the dress rehearsals wore on, he managed once to fall precisely on the last count of the music. A second attempt was also successful. Anderson then asked him to try it again, "for luck."[25] On the third attempt the safety latch gave way and Vabanque hurtled to the bare floor. Anderson raced to the cage and pulled the performer out. Fortunately for both men, the lions were old and nearly toothless. Vabanque survived, but never recovered sufficiently to work at his trade again. Despite such risks, the number was retained in the show and a second aerialist managed to perform it throughout the run without mishap.

Less dramatic problems also began to develop. The finale, an elaborate circus wedding with all the animals and performers on-stage, was a disaster the first time it was attempted. The animals had previously been rehearsed only in small groups. No one had anticipated that many of them had a natural antipathy toward one another. In fact, most of the beasts went into a frenzy when asked to share the ring with so many other species. The llamas kicked, the pigs screamed, and the reindeer shook Raoul Pène duBois's miniature top hats and veils from their antlers. "Only a pair of monkeys tripped around the arena," Anderson recalled, "apparently enthralled by Mr. Wagner's *Wedding March.*"[26]

The animals' diverse temperaments created other problems as well. During the final two weeks of rehearsal, Big Rosie developed a cold. Every time she sneezed, the llama preceding her in the opening parade stopped and brought the entire procession to a halt. The lambs trained to lie down next to a lion kept expiring from fright. "The mortality rate in lambs is so high," Maney observed, "that we don't know if Whitney can stand it."[27]

Even Anderson's run-of-the-mill instructions were unusual. "All right now!" he bellowed at one rehearsal. "The bandwagon will follow the calliope, then the llamas and the donkeys and the white horse on the right. The black bear is wheeled off first. And will the lady with the dromedary move a few steps forward. All right, is everybody standing by?"[28]

The complexity of the staging and the logistical nightmare involved with coordinating so many different acts into a well-timed production led to numerous delays. Originally scheduled to debut at the end of August or early in September, *Jumbo* soon became one of the most postponed shows in Broadway history. The premiere was rescheduled seven times in eleven weeks. Richard Maney made the most of these delays with frequent satiric updates on the show's progress and problems. He had the side of the Hippodrome adorned with a huge sign that read: "SH-H-H-H! JUMBO IS IN REHEARSAL!" He also draped a similarly worded banner on the back of a smaller elephant and had the animal paraded up Sixth Avenue. The week the show actually opened, Maney had a line of six pachyderms trooping down Broadway. Although Rose never got permission for this stunt, no officials tried to stop it.[29]

Despite efforts to keep rehearsals closed, the run-throughs drew large crowds of curious theatre types. Since rehearsals often lasted until 4:00 A.M., many Broadway regulars would drop in after their shows or club engagements were over. "It was *the* thing to do after the late night clubs closed," observed Maney. Rubbernecking at *Jumbo* rehearsals became such a vogue diversion for celebrities that Joan Crawford and Franchot Tone frequented the Hippodrome during their honeymoon.[30] Charles MacArthur wryly suggested that the opening was delayed because not everyone in New York had seen the show yet. Hecht suggested that the final ad read: "GRAND RE-OPENING BY POPULAR DEMAND!"

The many postponements had their negative effects, however. In order to get *Jumbo* posters displayed around town, Rose gave out hundreds of tickets to local merchants, allowing them to see the show anytime in October. When the opening was rescheduled to the middle of November, irate shop owners nearly stormed Rose's offices. Sensing a public relations disaster, he gave the complaining merchants new tickets.

Meanwhile, to offset the mounting preproduction costs, Rose offered to give a private full dress rehearsal for one person for $10,000. Maney had a wealthy distiller lined up when the Alcohol Control Board in Washington convinced Rose and Maney to call it off. The government felt that prohibitionists would reemerge in force if a liquor magnate flashed his profits in public.[31]

Rose did manage to bring in some extra revenue ($12,000 a week) by selling the radio serialization rights for *Jumbo* to Texaco, which planned to air segments of it weekly. When delays began to mount, Texaco insisted on starting the series whether the stage version was ready or not. Rose consented, and on October 29, more than two weeks before the actual premiere, Texaco broadcast the first of its programs. Durante and others in the cast performed material that was ultimately cut before the stage opening. Hecht and MacArthur padded the existing dialogue and revived deleted sections to provide most of the radio material.

Each episode began with a wailing fire engine siren, which was the oil company's radio signature. Shortly after the first installment, a *Jumbo* rehearsal was disrupted when Big Rosie decided to relieve herself on-stage.

Outside, a police siren screamed up Sixth Avenue. Durante listened to it, looked down at the immense puddle in the middle of the ring and intoned, "Texaco is on the air!"[32]

When the show opened on November 17, the major New York dailies and the trade papers carried an affidavit signed by Rose, declaring that *Jumbo* would indeed open that night. Still, there were doubters. A current revue had Rip Van Winkle awaken in 1975 and inquire, "Has *Jumbo* opened yet?"[33]

The first performance was a gala the likes of which Broadway had seldom seen. Droves of celebrities and show business notables paid from $25 to $200 to see the long-awaited spectacle. Sixth Avenue was closed north to Fifty-ninth Street, causing a traffic jam that delayed the curtain by nearly an hour. The audience roster rivaled the Oscars: Tallulah Bankhead, the Gershwins, Jack Dempsey, Irving Berlin, the Marx Brothers, Katharine Hepburn, Helen Hayes and scores of other big names. Fanny Brice appeared in a sleek black dress with a silver fox cape and a diamond she described as "big enough to stop a Cartier clock."[34]

In the midst of this chaos, Rose appeared calm and remained downstairs receiving the encouragement of well-wishers. When questioned about how he felt, Rose responded with a phrase Maney had composed for his program notes, "I stand on the Rubicon rattling the dice." Some journalists were so impressed with his fractured Caesar that they printed it the following day in their reviews. Rose had absolutely no idea what it meant, but he liked the way it sounded. "What the hell has a rubicon got to do with a crap game?" he asked Maney.[35]

John Murray Anderson chose to station himself backstage. His vantage point was adjacent to what the cast and crew referred to as the "cash box." This was a receptacle designed to receive the doings of any of the animals who might forget themselves during the course of the show. In the great rush for opening night seats, extra chairs had been placed at the edge of the proscenium. One bejewelled dowager who sat there on opening night was but a few feet from the "cash box." During one sequence this proximity proved unfortunate. "The dowager raised her lorgnette and leaned forward," Anderson recalled. "Suddenly, from out of the misty blue sea of light, both the dowager and I received a shovelful of 'cash' right in our faces."[36]

The lights dimmed, and *Jumbo* began with a brief fanfare. Rose hated overtures, believing that they were of interest "only to the composer's mother."[37] Instead of launching immediately into a splashy production number, he played on curiosity about the behind-the-scenes workings of a circus. The opening sequence focused on the laborious rehearsing and preparation required of circus performers. It also served to comment on and explain *Jumbo*'s seemingly endless preparation time.

The scene began with performers and musicians entering in street clothes and going through their acts. A group of tumblers made a mess of their landing. A clown walked by and remarked, "Not so good boys, you'll have to do it over." Similar critiques were offered as additional actors filled the stage. Horses appeared and circled the outside of the ring. A girl fired from a cannon landed in the arms of her partner. The ringmaster chided her, "Not so good my lass, you'll have to do it over." The ensemble picked up this refrain and turned it into the show's first song, "Over and Over Again."

The pace picked up as performers changed into their costumes. The girl in the cannon was relaunched and sailed precariously close to the audience before her partner (now seated in the front row) leapt up and caught her. Just as she landed, an aerialist in the balcony gripped a pulley with her teeth and slid down a three-hundred-foot wire to the stage. A drumroll signaled the entrance of Paul Whiteman on a magnificent white horse, followed by his orchestra in colorful marching band attire. The portly Whiteman had balked at this stunt until Rose offered to make a present of the Arabian if Whiteman rode it for the entrance. The band leader agreed, looking nervous but triumphant as he waved a gold baton. The audience gave him a standing ovation.[38]

This flourish led into the first production number and the second of many noteworthy Rodgers and Hart songs, "The Circus is on Parade." The show then settled down to introduce the principals and the Hecht-MacArthur story. The rival circus owners Mulligan and Considine feuded, while their progeny (Donald Novis and Gloria Grafton) met and immediately fell in love. Later in the act, Novis and Grafton's duets gave the show two of its prettiest songs, "The Most Beautiful Girl in the World" and "My Romance."[39]

Durante's appearance as Considine's flamboyant press agent, Claudius B. Bowers, gave *Jumbo* perhaps its single funniest scene. After the Considine show was put on the auction block, Durante tried to sneak away with Big Rosie. In the center of the ring he was stopped by a U.S. marshal who asked where Durante was going with the elephant. Unruffled, Durante glanced to either side and deadpanned, "What elephant?" It was the biggest laugh on two words in many years. As Maney pointed out, the gag only cost Jock Whitney a quarter of a million dollars to stage.[40]

The first act concluded with a lavish dream sequence. The circus had just been sold. Mickey Considine (Grafton) cries alone in the center of the ring. The lights dim except for a single spotlight focused on her as she weeps. A tiny silver carriage driven by a midget and pulled by four small ponies enters the ring. A little girl in blue, representing the heroine as a child, steps out to console Mickey, leading into the beautiful ballad, "Little Girl Blue." The little girl then tells Mickey, "They can't take the circus away from you because it's not under any canvas. The circus is in your heart." At this point out come clowns in rhinestones and silver, spangled stilt walkers, jugglers, aerialists and equestriennes. A glittering circus pageant develops as a fifty-foot papier-mâché clown is flown in to straddle the stage and bring the act to a close (fig. 9).[41]

The second act wisely featured the circus virtuosos and kept the sugar-coated plot in the background. Veteran headliners included the equestrienne Josie DeMotte (who starred with Barnum fifty years before), and the show's featured clown, A. Robins, who specialized in pulling huge stalks of bananas out of his jacket. Robins had come to American vaudeville from Europe in 1912.[42]

One of the second act's highlights was a number entitled "Memories of Madison Square Garden," in which an actor playing P. T. Barnum does a barker routine for an old-time circus. In front of a re-creation of the old Madison Square Garden exterior, the specialty acts went through their paces. There were fire eaters and other exotic acts from "Small Time Cavalcade" and enough trained animals and daredevil circus stunts for any serious big-top fan. Lions cavorted in a roofless cage while acrobats performed on a wire immediately above the beasts' heads. Dohoes, an educated white horse from Copenhagen, stood on his hind legs and applauded the goings on.[43]

The show closed, predictably, with the marriage of Mickey Considine and Matt Mulligan. This was "The Circus Wedding," for which Anderson had tried for six weeks to keep the animals in line. On opening night, the scene worked perfectly. As Novis and Grafton slowly rose above the ring in a garlanded porch swing, the cast and complete menagerie paraded below. The Allan Foster Girls also dangled overhead doing acrobatics and elaborate poses inside six-foot gymnastic rings (fig. 10).[44]

At 11:15 P.M. the cast took its bows. In the basement John Murray Anderson performed the peculiar personal ritual that marked the opening of every show he directed. Anderson took off the old blue suit he had worn every day for the six months that *Jumbo* rehearsed. After donning a new outfit, he set fire to the old one and remarked to Allan Foster, "I got mighty tired of that pin-stripe blue worsted."[45]

The general reaction to *Jumbo,* however, was anything but tired. The press was awash in a flood of superlatives. Percy Hammond of the *Tribune* declared it "a new and startling form of drama" and said of Rose: "If and when better big shows are built, he will build them."[46] Brooks Atkinson was delighted, calling *Jumbo* "perfect... a gargantuan antic, a paradise of bizarre and plain enjoyment."[47] Gilbert Gabriel of the *New York American* noted that "at least one backer left with a balloon in the shape of Jimmy Durante's schnozzle tied to his silk hat... we've none of us ever quite seen the like of it before.... [*Jumbo*] deserves endowment as an institution."[48]

Figure 9. Act 1 Finale of *Jumbo*, New York Hippodrome, 1935
(Courtesy Billy Rose Theatre Collection, New York Public Library, Astor, Lenox and Tilden Foundations)

44   Jumbo

Figure 10. Finale of *Jumbo*, New York Hippodrome, 1935
(Courtesy Billy Rose Theatre Collection, New York Public Library, Astor, Lenox and Tilden Foundations)

Billboard's Eugene Burr outdid even Maney's most flamboyant press releases. "There is no use in using superlatives to describe the production that Mr. Rose has furnished after his months of travail, the production that has stepped like Venus full-formed from his brow, after his aeons of gargantuan theatrical childbirth," he began. "Call it just a show—but take into consideration all those things that the word 'show' really means. *Jumbo* has all those things. Words such as 'colossal,' 'tremendous' and 'mammoth' fade into pallid insignificance before it. It is, gentlemen, a show!"[49]

But *Jumbo*'s success was not without adverse side effects. Almost as soon as the papers christened it a smash, questions arose as to whether Hecht and MacArthur had stolen the show's plot from a number of other works, most notably a piece entitled *Polly of the Circus*. After the radio series began, several authors stepped forward to insist that *Jumbo* was pirated from *Polly* and several obscure Hungarian plays, including the production that Rose had seen in Budapest. While none of these claims resulted in cash settlements, they did come back to haunt Rose. Hecht, who was angry over last-minute changes in the script, used doubts about its origins to get back at Rose. While Rose was negotiating the film rights with MGM, Hecht told the studio that he and MacArthur had indeed lifted the story from a Hungarian play. Originally prepared to pay Rose's asking price of $200,000, MGM settled with him for $50,000.

Another curious situation arose when Earl Carroll filed an injunction to stop the show, claiming that it "held him up to ridicule and contempt." The bone of contention was a sign Rose placed over the Hippodrome stage entrance that read: "THROUGH THESE PORTALS PASS THE MOST BEAUTIFUL ELEPHANTS IN THE WORLD!" While the play on the famous line in the *Vanities*' programs was obvious, Carroll's injunction was thrown out by the judge. Although Rose later removed the sign, he continued to refer to all things disorderly and unformed as looking like "the inside of Earl Carroll's stomach."[50]

Before it closed, *Jumbo* played 233 performances for more than one million people. Rose then moved the show to Texas for the Fort Worth Centennial from July to September of 1936. Although it was a success by most conventional Broadway standards, the show never recovered its enormous investment, estimated in the end to be nearly $350,000. Despite healthy profits from the Fort Worth run, Jock Whitney ended up losing close to $100,000. It may not have broken him, but it did make Billy Rose.[51]

Although some have suggested that Rose was drawn to spectacle because of its potentially huge profits, *Jumbo*'s tremendous losses make this contention hard to accept. Even had the show sold out its entire run, it would only have been slightly in the black.[52] More likely, it was the challenge of doing something others thought impossible that attracted him. The greater the scale of the project and the greater its apparent risks, the more he seemed to relish it. Maney's "little guy against the world" press image was more than just a convenient public persona; it was part and parcel of the way that Billy Rose saw himself. Since the newspapers had given him the mantle of Barnum, Rose was determined to make it fit.

Jumbo's popularity quelled Rose's envy of "serious" theatre that had led to *The Great Magoo* fiasco. He now realized that the standards of conventional theatre no longer applied to the shows he wanted to do. Now there were other traditions and techniques from which he could construct his hybrid extravaganzas. Rose's study of earlier spectacle producers had convinced him that their legacy was his future. In *Jumbo* Rose wedded the outdoor amusement tradition of Barnum and Buffalo Bill Cody to the indoor spectacle tradition of the Kiralfys and David Belasco. For good measure, he added elements from Broadway musical comedy, vaudeville and the nightclubs. The result was a synthesis of popular entertainment traditions that his earlier enterprises had anticipated but never completely achieved. It was a prime example of Rose's talent for combining traditional popular forms into new and seemingly novel entertainments.

For Rose, the most important result of *Jumbo* was his arrival as an independent and powerful figure in show business. He had come a long way from the nightclub owner whom Richard Maney described as "smoldering in the shadow of Fanny Brice." Rose's newly earned reputation as a producer of spectacle left him with the expectations of a press and public that wondered what he could possibly do to surpass this latest triumph. But they had little time to ponder, for chance was about to intervene and answer the question. In retrospect, it was all perfectly logical. What could be more fitting than a project involving Billy Rose and a group of Texas millionaires?

4

Fort Worth

On March 1, 1936, Rose flew to Hollywood, where he hoped to conclude a motion picture deal with MGM for *Jumbo*. He also wanted to spend time with Brice, who was working on *The Great Ziegfeld,* a movie biography of her late employer. For the past several years their relationship had suffered the vicissitudes of two successful but divergent careers. Rose was anxious to mend what he called "a marriage only the phone company could love."[1]

He also wanted to find a money-making project. Despite his enfant terrible image on Broadway, Rose's four New York productions had suffered combined losses of nearly $300,000. When he began musing in the press about a new show for the 1936–1937 season, George S. Kaufman commented that "Failure has gone to his head."[2] Normally fearless, Rose quaked at being labeled a squanderer of other people's money. His producing career would end quickly if such a reputation took hold.

Brice pressed him to remain in Hollywood. Life on the coast suited her, and she felt that Rose could easily find success there as a producer. She rightly sensed that unless one of them settled down, the marriage was doomed. Rose knew things were amiss but expected his wife to make the concessions. He could not accept the fact that she refused to stay home and become Mrs. Rose. It was a conflict that their usual affability and deep friendship never overcame. Years later, she said of him: "Billy was a little boy very much in love with the sandbox he was in. He never figured out why I didn't want to stay and play with him in it."[3]

Still the unflappable optimist, Rose thought he could save the marriage while engineering his next career move. Visiting Brice on the MGM lot one day, he took a shortcut through the courtyard of the studio's Executive Building. Halfway across, he heard his name shouted from a window on the second floor. It was Rufus Le Maire, then an MGM casting director. Le Maire asked him up to his office.

Seeing Rose from his window solved one of Le Maire's biggest casting dilemmas. Several days before, he had received a call from Amon Carter, the leading citizen in his hometown of Fort Worth. Carter, the town's wealthiest landowner and publisher of the major Fort Worth newspaper, had a problem. The city's nearby rival Dallas had been selected as the site for the upcoming Texas Centennial. This was a particularly galling development to Carter, who, when forced to visit Dallas at mealtime, always carried a sack lunch so as not to spend any money there. He also made certain that none of the Dallas newspapers carried the weekly column of his good friend Will Rogers. The Centennial decision was more than he could bear.

Refusing to be upstaged, Carter and several other wealthy civic boosters decided to mount a rival exposition. They had already acquired a site for the project and even engineered a large bond sale. Plans had been made for Indian craft displays and agricultural exhibits. Now they needed someone to create a miracle on the prairie and build a fair to steal Dallas's thunder. Carter called Le Maire, one of the few people from Fort Worth with extensive show business connections. Although anxious to accommodate one of Texas's most powerful men, Le Maire also experienced a desire peculiar to Fort Worth natives: outdoing Dallas. He told Carter he would find someone for the job.

Until he spied Rose in the courtyard, however, Le Maire was stymied. Now it seemed that the solution had appeared under his nose. Le Maire described the job with all the enthusiasm he could muster. Rose was cool to the idea and told Le Maire, "It sounds like some sort of carnival proposition to me."[4] Le Maire persisted and finally convinced Rose to think it over and see him again in a day or two. After Rose left his office, Le Maire telephoned Fort Worth. Carter and a number of other Fort Worth businessmen had seen *Jumbo* in New York and heartily agreed with Le Maire's choice. As for Rose's reluctance to take the job, Carter assured Le Maire it was no problem. A friend in New York would take care of everything.

Several hours later, Rose received a call from Jock Whitney, who strongly suggested that he fly to Texas and discuss the job with Carter. Rose and Le Maire were on a plane to Fort Worth the following morning. It was Rose's first experience with the long arm of Amon Carter, whom Rose soon learned "really had all the intimate friends Elsa Maxwell talks about having."[5]

Carter and the other members of the exposition's board met Rose and Le Maire at the airport and drove them to the site. Fort Worth was hot and dry, even in March, and the whole town seemed suffused with dust and heat. Rose squinted at the desolate surroundings as Carter talked glowingly about how the city had raised $500,000 for its fair. When Rose asked about Dallas's budget, the wind went out of Amon Carter's sails; Dallas had already earmarked $25,000,000 for the centennial and secured most of the available corporate and international exhibitors.

Arriving at the site, Rose received another shock. He stepped out of the car onto 140 acres of naked prairie, broken only by tumbleweeds and an occasional mesquite tree. After making obligatory comments about the location's lack of water, sewage and electricity, Rose experienced the greatest shock of all: the barons of Fort Worth wanted a functioning fair on the wasteland in three months.

Rose was stunned but intrigued. Only men with enormous audacity and resources could believe such a thing possible. Though he had known them scarcely two hours, Rose felt at ease with the homespun bluster of these Texas millionaires. They were ready for anything and afraid of nothing. For once he had found a group whose braggadocio surpassed his own.

After a repast of Texas beef at the Fort Worth Athletic Club, Rose's hosts asked the fateful question. Rose winked at Le Maire and asked for an hour to himself. The club's maître d' showed him to a windowless writing room equipped with a small portable typewriter. Rose sat down and in less than forty-five minutes typed what, with few changes, became the plan for the Fort Worth Centennial. The first step would be to pack up *Jumbo* in its entirety and transport it to Fort Worth. Next he would build a frontier-style saloon and put on an outdoor wild west show with music. He also suggested a huge open-air café with a stage show that would play to an audience of 10,000. To round out the wild west theme, Rose proposed a complete Western town featuring concessions, exhibits and souvenirs. He rejoined the committee and began to outline his plans.

Rose's first question was about the weather. Hearing that hundred-degree days were the rule in July, he suggested that the fair operate only in the evening and on weekends. He then went right to the heart of the matter. "Make it strictly a cabaret fair, an entertainment exposition," he suggested. "You haven't got any industrial exhibitors that amount to a damn anyway." Rose went on to deflate most of the committee's ideas for the fair.

> All this wigwam handicraft nonsense is out. The only way to compete with $25,000,000 worth of industrial technology is with pelvic technology. We have to give them girls and more girls. Your only chance of bucking Dallas is entertainment on a grand scale, with a strong Western flavor, but meeting big-time standards in every way... we don't hire Joe Blow and his Melody Five, we hire Paul Whiteman."[6]

Le Maire glanced around the table. The Fort Worthies, as Rose later called them, were captivated. Rose was in fine form. He suggested a statewide beauty contest to select girls for the exposition's various entertainments and to generate interest in the fair. In a state where people often drove a hundred miles or more to attend a dance, such publicity was vital. He closed out the presentation with a line that brought the city's boosters to their feet. Following through on his theme of an entertainment-oriented fair, Rose coined the slogan "Dallas for Education, Fort Worth for Entertainment." The millionaires shouted their approval. It was perfect: they would hoist Dallas on its own pretentious petard.

The Texans hardly blinked when Rose told them that the project would cost nearly two million dollars and lose at least half that much. "You can't build what amounts to a small town and expect to amortize it in 90 days," he told them. "But if you see it as a civic promotion, it will pay big dividends. Look at it this way: You may lose a million, but Dallas stands to lose 25."[7]

Carter and the other members of the committee were suitably inspired and asked what sort of remuneration Rose expected. Without hesitation, Rose told them $100,000. Le Maire was shocked. He had assumed the city might offer $25,000 or $30,000 at best. The committee asked to consider the proposition in private. After a brief discussion, with Rose pacing the hall and Le Maire berating him for undue greed, Carter emerged and shook Rose's hand. The exposition board had agreed to pay him more than $1000 a day between then and the fair's scheduled opening. Showing up Dallas would not be cheap.

To the uninitiated, the feud between Dallas and Fort Worth was a curious and inexplicable bit of regional folklore. In point of fact, the two cities were far more different than a distance of thirty miles would indicate. While each possessed the gargantuan pride and insecurity unique to Texas, their personalities were as night and day. Fort Worth was firmly rooted in the cattle and oil dominions of west Texas. It had evolved into a flourishing commercial center as the junction of the cattle trails and the railroad. Even in 1936 it maintained the rough, unreconstructed air of a frontier town. Fort Worth's residents looked with pride on its nickname of "Cowtown"; they liked to think of their city as the place "where the West begins." Dallas, on the other hand, was a town of merchants and bankers that considered itself a cultured and sophisticated metropolis. It was, for Texas, a very Eastern city, conscious of urban fashions and leery of its rowdy neighbor to the west.

Many Texans were shocked when the legislature selected Dallas as the official site for the state centennial. How could this sissified town begin to honor Sam Houston, Davy Crockett and the other Texas heroes? Surely San Antonio with its Alamo or Houston, the site of Santa Anna's defeat, would be more appropriate. Dallas did not even exist in 1836.

The truth was that Dallas simply outbid everyone else. The city's leading banker, Robert Thornton, went to Austin and proudly announced, "We've got the money, and to show our pride in Texas, we've got the guts to spend it."[8] Thornton told the legislature that Dallas was prepared to spend $12,000,000 of its own money on buildings and grounds, in addition to nearly $10,000,000 guaranteed by exhibitors. To a state suspicious of any government expenditure, it was too good a deal to pass up. To Amon Carter, it was an outrage.

That Fort Worth should choose Billy Rose to create its exposition is hardly surprising. Ever since Little Egypt titillated the Columbian Exposition in 1893, world's fairs and expositions had evolved into highly theatrical entertainments. From static displays of agricultural and manufactured goods, they had become festive entertainments more akin to carnivals than the stately exhibitions typified by London's Crystal Palace.

To be sure, world's fairs were still exercises in cultural vanity and self-promotion, and like any mass celebration or festival they provided ample opportunities for profit. They were costly to stage, however, and required large, free-spending audiences to survive. Performers, food-and-drink concessions and mechanized amusements were needed to enliven the proceedings and provide a steady cash flow. Despite the increasing presence of light entertainment, few major international or regional expositions managed to break even, let alone show a profit.

A recent exception had been the Chicago Century of Progress Exposition of 1933. The likelihood that a major fair would succeed in the depths of the Depression seemed scant. But people flocked to it, as they did to the fantasy-laden films and musicals of the day. Rose's New York productions had also pandered to this need for escape, but never on such a scale as the Chicago Exposition. For a few hours, fair visitors could forget the dreary state of the world and wander through a vista of marvelous exhibits and entertainments.

In addition to the usual displays by corporations and foreign exhibitors, Chicago had presented a wide variety of unusual entertainments. There was Mona Leslie, a lady clothed "only in a coat of silver paint," who dived into a pool of vivid blue water and performed dances that fair officials described as "no more immoral than the nudes at the Art Institute."[9] Faith Bacon also performed and was forced to withdraw one number from her repertoire. In "Sigh of the Cross," Bacon hung nude on a crucifix and undulated to the strains of Ravel's "Boléro." Ava Gardner and Sally Rand (the former Helen Gould Beck) also caused a stir with their exotic striptease routines. Rand was once arrested three times in a single day.

Other risqué activities included an actual nudist wedding held at Sinclair's dinosaur diorama. The participants included eight nude couples and a pastor in a goatskin loincloth. The nudity craze continued in the Mexican Village, whose "Aztec Sacrifice" featured an unclad "virgin leaping to her death in a cauldron of flame." Not to be outdone, the Hawaii Garden presented "The Slave Who Dared," in which a naked maiden was killed at each show by a fire spewing Buddha.[10]

The side-show flavor of the fair also took less prurient but equally bizarre forms. There was a new kind of baseball played on the backs of donkeys and a naval battle in Lake Michigan. A fully inhabited midget village (with forty-five tiny buildings and miniature cars) offered a midget production of *Floradora*. Robots made their first appearance at a world's fair with such notable automatons as Chief Pontiac, who entertained visitors at the GM

Pavilion: "He carries on a conversation, answers questions, and will tell you anything you want to know about the new Pontiac Straight Eight. He likes particularly to chat with old Pontiac owners about the long satisfactory service their cars are giving."[11]

The increasingly carnivalesque character of such expositions appealed to Rose, who knew that similar foolery had made his New York nightclubs a success. He was becoming quite adept at creating spectacular productions from the tried and true ingredients of vaudeville, burlesque and musical comedy. That particular mixture of novelty, naughtiness and nostalgia was central to Rose's concept of entertainment. The popularity of the Chicago fair served to confirm his instincts. If funny acts, crazy stunts and girls could salvage cabarets and world's fairs, they would probably do the same for Fort Worth.[12]

Rose had the advantage of working for men whose penchant for the outlandish equaled his own. The exuberantly tasteless collection of entertainments he envisioned perfectly suited Amon Carter and his associates. They did not particularly care what Rose did as long as it drew attention to Fort Worth and crowds away from Dallas. When Rose warned Carter that most of the entertainments were not family fare, he replied breezily, "Our children are extremely precocious." If Chicago could get away with mechanical Indians, midgets and naked ladies, anything was possible in Fort Worth.

Rose wasted little time organizing his staff for the Fort Worth Centennial. He cabled John Murray Anderson who was vacationing in Paris and asked if Anderson could leave immediately. The following day, Rose received a two-word reply: "Have left."[13] He also managed to secure the participation of the rest of his *Jumbo* staff. Albert Johnson designed not only the productions and performance spaces but the rest of the fair's buildings and landscaping as well. Raoul Pène duBois agreed to create the costumes and Robert Alton the choreography. Carlton Winckler, Anderson's lighting designer and technical director, was given the considerable task of devising the lighting and electrical scheme for the entire fair. Rose decided to write the lyrics for the cabaret piece and hired young Dana Suese (who had composed the popular "You Ought to Be in Pictures") to write the music.

To provide the right kind of publicity, Rose brought Ned Alvord to Fort Worth and convinced the fair committee to allocate him $80,000 for promotional activities. This included covering the state's highways with billboards depicting a curvaceous cowgirl and Rose's slogan, "Dallas for Education, Fort Worth for Entertainment." Alvord erected a huge neon sign opposite the entrance to the Dallas Fair that read, "Forty Minutes to Fort Worth and Whoppee!"[14] He also supervised the statewide beauty contests that were to provide comely girls, the most striking of whom would be crowned

Miss Texas Sweetheart. Alvord managed to bring Clark Gable to Texas to judge the finals of the contest. Faye Cotton, a shy girl who taught Sunday school in the oilfield town of Borger, won the contest and later starred in the fair's elaborate cabaret revue.

Carter and the fair committee gave Rose a $25,000 advance on his salary and a large downtown office. With only nine weeks to cast and rehearse five live shows, activity was feverish. Brooks Costume of New York opened a Fort Worth branch in an old overall factory to handle the fair's $40,000 costume budget. Albert Johnson finished working drawings of the entire fair in less than a week. Excavation and construction began even before local architects had converted his designs into blueprints.

Most of the efforts centered on the fair's two primary entertainments, the huge outdoor cabaret and Rose's musical wild west show. Rose had wanted to call the cabaret Casa Diavolo, after the trapeze–lion act sequence from *Jumbo*. John Murray Anderson thought it too grim and came up with the theatre's ultimate name, Casa Mañana (House of Tomorrow).

Rose liked the image of a show years ahead of its time, and Ned Alvord immediately began heralding it as "decades beyond anything else in the world." But despite the novel title, Rose and Anderson began outlining a thoroughly conventional revue based on the theme of world's fairs past and present. The show was modeled along the lines of earlier cabaret productions at Casino de Paree and the Billy Rose Music Hall, albeit somewhat grander and on a more elaborate scale.

Johnson's design for this open air theatre restaurant was a huge amphitheatre colonnaded with two levels of Moorish arches in the style of the Alcazar. It was a curious piece of theatrical architecture, part bullring, part Roman naumachia (figs. 11 & 12). Pathways leading to the arena were lined with shade trees and fountains. Inside were tiered concentric circles of tables leading down to a revolving stage 130 feet in diameter that floated back and forth over a miniature lake as it turned. Rose's original idea was to have the audience revolve around the stage, but this proved far too complex and expensive. Stage engineer Richard Bruckner designed the 1500-ton aquatic turntable and its elaborate hydraulic and mechanical controls, which required a crew of twelve to operate. The theatre accommodated 4500 for dinner and another 3000 in balcony seats behind the colonnades.[15] On seeing the completed Casa Mañana, a New York journalist said, "It was like finding Radio City in the middle of the Gobi Desert."[16]

The preparations for the wild west show, "The Last Frontier," were similarly monumental. The pageant was to depict the history of Texas from the earliest Spanish explorers to the present day. Lacking suitable terrain for a natural amphitheatre, Albert Johnson had bulldozers and steam shovels create several hills against which to stage the spectacle and seat an audience of

Figure 11. Model of Theatre in Casa Mañana, Fort Worth, 1936
(Courtesy Billy Rose Theatre Collection, New York Public Library, Astor, Lenox and Tilden Foundations)

10,000 (fig. 13). Anderson and Rose collected 400 rodeo performers, Indians and stunt men, in addition to a cast of 600 dancers and singers. For the finale, Robert Alton choreographed a square dance with 300 couples whom duBois costumed in four different colors.[17]

At the conclusion of the dance, a herd of buffalo were to stampede down one of the artificial mountains. This proved to be as difficult as securing the cooperation of the animals in the *Jumbo* finale. Unlike circus animals, buffalo were not available in captivity. Thirty-six were captured at the King Ranch and loaded on boxcars to Fort Worth. Before they could be herded into trucks at the Fort Worth railroad yard, however, the beasts escaped and cavorted down Main Street. Alvord made the most of this mishap in the newspapers the following day: "BRUTISH BISONS CAROUSE IN COWTOWN!" screamed one headline.[18]

The animals did prove difficult to manage. They were noisy, totally untrained, and smelled like a truckload of rotten meat. Since these qualities

Figure 12. Audience as Seen from the Stage in Casa Mañana, Fort Worth, 1936
(Courtesy Billy Rose Theatre Collection, New York Public Library, Astor, Lenox and Tilden Foundations)

were unalterable, provisions had to be made to conceal them from the audience until the finale. A large tunnel was bored under the mountain so that the buffalo could be led from off-stage pens to the rear of the hill down which they were to stampede. Keeping them in the tunnel during the show also masked most of the odor and noise.

Emerging from the tunnel, the buffalo ran along a fenced corridor to the top of the hill and raced to the bottom, where mounted cowboys herded them into a corral. Timing the stampede was critical, for once it began, there was no stopping it. Carlton Winckler, who ran the light and stage cues from a central console, had to signal the release of the buffalo, as the stagehands in the tunnel could neither see nor hear the show. This made rehearsals difficult, for once the animals had run down the hill, they refused to be crowded back into the tunnel for a second try. Anderson, normally a stickler for repetition, had to be satisfied with only three stampedes prior to the opening.[19]

The fair's other attractions were also beginning to take shape. To house the transplanted and slightly reduced *Jumbo* company, Johnson built an enclosed circular building of redwood and wrought iron modeled after the Hippo Cirque, a New York spectacle house that once stood across from the

Figure 13. *The Last Frontier*, Fort Worth, 1936
(Courtesy Billy Rose Theatre Collection, New York Public Library, Astor, Lenox and Tilden Foundations)

Academy of Music on Fourteenth Street.[20] Carlton Winckler restaged the show as a ninety-minute presentation that kept only the barest outlines of the plot. Although Big Rosie and most of the animals were included, *Jumbo* was without the services of Jimmy Durante. Eddie Foy played Durante's part in Fort Worth, and a young Texan named Wyn Cahoon took over the Gloria Grafton role.[21]

Johnson also designed The Sunset Trail, a Western town patterned after the midway at the 1893 Columbian Exposition. Just as the Chicago fair had placed re-created foreign villages on either side of a wide promenade, The Sunset Trail arranged typical buildings of an 1870s frontier town along a gas-lit dirt trail (fig. 14). Like its famous predecessor, the town attempted to re-create the more flamboyant activities of its inhabitants. There were gunfights, barroom brawls, stagecoach and bank robberies and a host of other colorful events. As in Rose's original plan, there was a saloon offering Gay Nineties showgirl routines and honky-tonk piano music.

Figure 14. The Sunset Trail, Fort Worth, 1936
(Courtesy Billy Rose Theatre Collection, New York Public Library, Astor, Lenox and Tilden Foundations)

An even more elaborate show took place at the Pioneer Palace, which featured Lulu Bates performing such numbers as "You're So Beautiful It Hurts" and "Striptease Susie." Tom Patricola, a veteran tap dancer (who had appeared with George White's *Scandals*), performed on top of a forty-foot bar, whose large mirror retracted to provide additional stage space. An added touch of frontier realism occurred one evening when a locust flew into Bates's mouth while she was attempting a particularly high note. According to Anderson, she kept on singing, although "slightly off key."[22]

In addition to Bates and Patricola, the Palace offered what was by now a Rose signature act, the Rosebuds. In this version, Robert Alton choreographed ballet routines for six female dancers whose combined weight totaled 1,360 pounds. There were other performers from the "Small Time Cavalcade," including Eddie Eddy the cry artist, the fire-eating Magfys, and the Melba Sisters, who played xylophone renditions of cowboy ballads on a row of whiskey bottles.

One of the more popular concessions was operated by Sally Rand, who also appeared in the Casa Mañana show. Her Nude Ranch was precisely what its name indicated. The show featured young ladies clad only in holsters, sombreros and boots. They performed a variety of Western stunts, including rope tricks, pistol twirling, and, of course, bareback riding.

Despite the huge task of preparing these myriad attractions, the Fort Worth Frontier Centennial only missed its target opening of July 4 by a week. Interest in the New York press was considerable. Richard Maney retired Rose's title of "Bantum Barnum" and rechristened him the "Al Fresco Frohman" in honor of Casa Mañana. Maney also released photographs of Rose in cowboy attire, as well as one of him giving an archery demonstration with two Indians. Fanny Brice was particularly amused and cabled Fort Worth: "One Hebe comic in the family is enough."[23]

Meanwhile in Dallas, the centennial's promoters were determined not to let Rose brand their event a stuffy pseudoeducational bore. While Rose lambasted Dallas as possessing "enough refinement to choke all the horses in the state," Texas's official fair quietly tripled its entertainment section's budget.[24] A Streets of Paris concession similar to the one at the 1933 Chicago Fair was added, and several Sally Rand–style fan dancers were booked. Although its promotion was not as vigorous, Dallas eventually had almost as many risqué acts as its self-proclaimed bawdy rival.

The Casa Mañana show was a week from opening when Rose and Anderson decided that it lacked a hit song. In a sequence that would be a cliché for anyone but Billy Rose, the two men went to Dana Suesse's hotel late that night and woke her up. The composer answered her door in bathrobe and curlers and told them to leave. Rose explained the need for a big song and pleaded, "But Dana, the night is young." Anderson added sarcastically, "and you're so beautiful." The phrases suddenly clicked in Rose's mind. He walked Suesse to the piano in her sitting room, and in less than an hour they fashioned the revue's best song, "The Night Is Young and You're So Beautiful."[25]

When the Fort Worth Frontier Centennial opened on July 11, the paint on the Casa Mañana scenery had barely dried, and stagehands were still refocusing lights less than an hour before the first show. Nevertheless, the revue ran smoothly. Anderson and Rose had wisely kept the production numbers simple and relied on duBois's lavish costumes and several impressive specialty acts to carry the day.

With Paul Whiteman's orchestra on one side of the stage and Joe Venuti's on the other, the revue began with a reprise of the St. Louis World's Fair of 1904. After renditions of period favorites such as "Meet Me in St. Louis, Louis" and "The Good Old Summer Time," Ann Pennington performed a *danse du ventre* (belly dance) reminiscent of Little Egypt. The St. Louis scene closed with Everett Marshall singing the last-minute Rose-Suesse composition, "The Night Is Young."

Raoul Pène duBois's costumes highlighted the next scene, which was set at the Paris Fair of 1925. The opening number, "You're in Paree," consisted of showgirls costumed as Parisian landmarks, the most inspired of which was Mary Dowell, a six-foot-two-inch Texas girl who appeared as Montmartre.[26] Rose's lyrics halfheartedly mimicked the phrasing of Cole Porter's "Anything Goes":

> You're in Paree, in gay Paree.
> If you wake up and you're connected
> With a breakfast partner unexpectedly,
> You're in Paree.[27]

A routine titled "Le Can-Can" attempted to capture the flavor of Parisian nightclubs by having its chorus enter atop a gigantic champagne bottle which popped its cork at the appropriate moment and spewed forth pink bubbles. The Paris scene concluded with a specialty dance by Gomez and Winoma, who were almost upstaged by the chorus's Eiffel Tower-shaped headgear.[28]

The third scene focused on the recent Chicago Century of Progress Exposition of 1933. Rose's lyrical association of sexual abandon with world's fair cities continued with "It Happened in Chicago":

> At the exposition there,
> I was eyeing up the fair,
> When along comes Mame, a classy dame,
> With golden teeth and platinum hair.
> I wines and dines her, but when I'm out o' cash,
> She grabs Handsome Joe with the black moustache.[29]

Sally Rand provided the highpoint of the scene by re-creating the fan dance that precipitated her arrest at the 1933 Chicago fair. She was accompanied by a corps de ballet draped in vividly colored ostrich feathers. The opulence of this sequence prompted one Fort Worth reviewer to wonder how the ungrateful critics of Chicago "failed to see Miss Rand's work for the supreme artistic achievement it is."[30]

The revue's fourth and final sequence, a series of tableaux entitled "A Masque of Texas," depicted the various peoples and nations that had ruled Texas throughout its history. Beginning with Indian canoes and a revolving Comanche village, the stage turned slowly to reveal the state's four hundred years of Anglo settlement through an elaborate costume parade. Each sequence offered a flamboyant sample of female dress in the relevant historical period, along with a uniformed soldier carrying the appropriate flag. This lavish bit of posing concluded with a display of present-day fashion by Miss Texas Sweetheart Faye Cotton, who appeared in a $10,000 gold mesh dress.

For the finale the great floating platform rejoined the lip of the auditorium for a spectacular dance number in which Ann Pennington displayed one of duBois's more elaborate creations as "The Girl in the Hundred Gallon Hat." The stage then parted from the front of the audience to reveal a slender lagoon. As the sliver of water widened, gondolas outlined in tiny lights and filled with topless chorus girls glided by on unseen wires. This brought the revue to a close as the crowd roared its approval.[31]

The members of the New York press whom Maney had flown to Fort Worth were exultant. But then, after a week of pampered all-expenses-paid treatment, they might well have applauded a turkey shoot. Yet Casa Mañana *was* an impressive piece of spectacle. Damon Runyon could find few comparisons in the realm of conventional theatre: "If you took the Polo Grounds and converted it into a café and then adopted the best scenic effects of an old-time Ziegfeld production, you might get something approximating Casa Mañana."[32]

Despite temperatures that often stayed in the eighties until nine o'clock at night, the Fort Worth Frontier Centennial drew large crowds. Although it did not totally overshadow the larger exposition in Dallas, the national publicity generated by the fair poured millions of dollars into the local economy and established Fort Worth as a "fun" town. Carter and other civic leaders were so pleased with Rose's efforts that they decided to operate the fair for a second season in 1937, under the new title "Fort Worth Frontier Fiesta."

To generate a fresh wave of publicity Richard Maney came up with a novel stunt. During intermissions at Casa Mañana the audience was invited to dance on-stage. Rose noted that there were few participants and soon learned that most Fort Worth men had little interest in or knowledge of the latest steps. He also knew that the gigolo system he employed at Casino de Paree would hardly be appropriate in Baptist Fort Worth. Maney suggested importing legitimate dancing partners in the form of displaced European noblemen.

Rose liked the idea, and Maney took out advertisements in the New York papers calling for applicants to submit "photographs with medals and attendants" and other suitable proof of peerage. He added that "sons of the Dauphin will receive short shrift."[33] Eventually, thirty-six titled young men were given travel expenses, a stipend, and room and board to spend a summer in Cowtown. The wealthy of Fort Worth loved the stunt and arranged a series of gala parties to welcome the visiting nobility. As Rose later noted, many of them "never used the other half of their plane ticket."[34]

Although most of the 1937 fair's features remained the same, Sally Rand's departure to tour the country with her Nude Ranch prompted Rose and Anderson to create a new Casa Mañana revue. The 1937 edition was a pageant built around the plots of the year's four best-selling novels: *Gone with the Wind, Lost Horizon, Wake Up and Live* and *It Can't Happen Here*. The result was four elaborate tableaux with music and choreography. Dialogue was eliminated, according to the program, to emphasize the show's "visual and melodic appeal."[35] Since Rand's absence diminished the burlesque element, Rose took a different tack and, on Robert Alton's recommendation, hired dancer Harriet Hoctor. Opera star Everett Marshall returned to sing the revue's principal songs.

The revue began with a huge cotillion sequence from *Gone with the Wind* and proceeded through the four novels with sets of increasingly monumental proportion. Albert Johnson constructed thirty-foot-high columns for the Tara sequence of *Gone with the Wind,* as well as a Tibetan monastery setting for *Lost Horizons* that stretched eighty-five feet across the stage and rose in levels to a height of forty-three feet.[36]

The finale enacted the cautionary anti-Fascist message of *It Can't Happen Here* with sixteen stage elevators and a flotilla of battleships steaming across the lagoon. The Junoesque Mary Dowell again appeared in a striking costume, this time as Miss Liberty with a 1200-yard train of spangled satin that required twenty-eight attendants to manipulate as she ascended a lofty flight of chromium stairs. The lyrics for this scene played on American fears about chaos in Europe and the increasing sentiment for isolationism and self-interest:

> Let cannon thunder over the sea,
> Let men be slaves who used to be free;
> Let Hell appear, but never fear—
> IT CAN'T HAPPEN HERE!
> Let men in black and crimson and brown,
> See all their hopes come tumbling down;...
> If we can guard our own backyard—
> IT JUST CAN'T HAPPEN OVER HERE![37]

While Rose's extravagant pageant was generally well-received by the public, others were less favorably impressed. Margaret Mitchell, who was then seeing her novel *Gone with the Wind* produced as a motion picture, claimed that no one had secured her permission to use elements of the book at Casa Mañana. Rose was forced to remove all references to specific characters and places (Tara became "a mansion"), and pay Mitchell several thousand dollars in damages. Luckily for Rose, none of the other authors felt an inclination to sue.

Rose's success at Fort Worth cemented the production team with whom he collaborated throughout the next decade. Anderson, Johnson, Alton and the others were to create their most popular productions with a man whom band leader Paul Whiteman once called "a certifiable lunatic. Only a nut like Billy Rose could conceive a show like this."[38]

Rose's schemes became all the more grandiose after he came to understand the potential of expositions. Here was a form of show business where budgets were practically unlimited, and producers seldom worried about the bottom line. Unlike circuses and other types of outdoor amusement, world's fairs were considered legitimate enterprises, quite distinct from the lowly world of big tops and carnivals. Rose realized that his recycled entertainments would lose their side show stigma when placed in the elevated environment of a great exposition.

He began to talk loftily of how Broadway was an inadequate forum for his productions and was rapidly losing its impact in the world of show business. "There are just three wealthy entertainment businesses: radio, motion pictures and expositions," he declared. "The theatre simply does not rate as a competitive factor in the entertainment industry.... Why should people go to see a show that costs a puny 10–20 thousand when they can see a film like *San Francisco* that cost a million?"[39]

Billy Rose was again thinking big, bigger, biggest. The use of aquatics at Casa Mañana had given him an idea. He wired Maney in New York: "Have a great idea for a new show. It all takes place in the water. Am negotiating for a small pier on the East River. Will need 500 actors who can swim. Does the ocean come under Equity?"[40]

5

Cleveland, 1937: The First *Aquacade*

The 1930s soon became the golden age of world's fairs. In addition to the Fort Worth, Dallas and Chicago fairs, major expositions were planned by New York, Paris, San Francisco, Vancouver, Glasgow, Cleveland and several other cities. To a world starved for good news, these glittering shows offered at least the hope of a better tomorrow. They provided both a respite from the Depression and a practical means of creating employment.

The potential for civic self-promotion was also considerable; expositions enabled even smaller cities to attract worldwide attention by providing the public with tangible samples of the exotic fare found in movies and newsreels. Despite advances in mass communication, world's fairs still constituted a significant dissolution of boundary and distance. At a time when few people had the means to travel beyond their immediate region, fairs offered visitors a variety of foreign and domestic entertainments in a single, carefully planned environment. For so practiced a purveyor of amusements as Billy Rose, the opportunities were obvious.

Rose's world's fair debut had been remarkably auspicious. Exposition planners came in droves to marvel at Casa Mañana's novel diversions and steady cash flow. Their interest in popular and profitable amusements was understandable. Most fairs operated only during the warmer months and needed spectacular entertainments to boost attendance and meet ongoing expenses. Fort Worth's emphasis on amusement provided a lesson future world's fairs took to heart.

The city of Cleveland paid particularly close attention to Rose's example. The Great Lakes Exposition had just closed its first season with attendance and income well below expectations. Cleveland had hoped to follow in the footsteps of Chicago's Century of Progress Exposition (see chapter 4), which had utilized a similar lakefront setting to great advantage. For its 1937 season, the fair's managers planned to completely revamp the amusement zone. They also decided to repaint the exposition's buildings in vivid colors similar to those used by Albert Johnson at Fort Worth and Josef Urban at the 1933

Chicago Fair. In a decade that was to produce some of history's most notable expositions, Cleveland wanted its fair to stand out from the crowd.

The Great Lakes Exposition was unique in that it was funded primarily by private subscriptions. But despite a declaration that "No public subsidy has been sought from federal, state, county or city government," the project received substantial assistance from the city.[1] More than $40,000,000 worth of municipal lakefront property was given to the Exposition for use during the fair. In return, the underwriters promised to assume all building and maintenance costs and present the city with a host of permanent improvements, including a new subway line on East Ninth Street.[2]

The goal of permanently developing portions of the site sapped much of the fair's available capital. Publicity and entertainment zone budgets were cut dramatically to reduce cost overruns. In their haste to satisfy city officials, the promoters slighted the festive qualities necessary for a popular fair. The drab buildings and grounds were devoid of the exuberant entertainment that had made Fort Worth a success. One local reviewer commented that Cleveland might be better off "selling tickets to a penal colony."[3]

The exposition's principal theatrical offering was a dreary pageant entitled *Parade of the Years,* which told the story of transportation with a monotonous display of period conveyances. Other exposition highlights included a demonstration of slum clearance procedures, a police fingerprinting bureau, and a $12,000 relief map of Cleveland built by Work Projects Administration workers.[4] General manager Lincoln Dickey sensed that radical changes would be required to revive the fair in 1937.

Dickey was a former Chautauqua lecturer who had once managed the convention hall in Atlantic City. He visited Casa Mañana in the fall of 1936 and knew immediately that Rose was the man Cleveland needed. Anyone who could build a successful fair on a desolate prairie in three months was worth talking to.

After some preliminary discussions, Rose flew to Cleveland on February 1, three months before the Exposition was scheduled to reopen. The site was boarded up and nearly deserted as Dickey and Rose walked around the grounds. Above the howling Lake Erie wind, Rose heard music coming over a loudspeaker. He followed it to a pier where a cast of three clowns, a diver and six chorus girls splashed about in the icy water. It was a rehearsal of the exposition's free water show.

It was strictly side-show fare, but Rose was fascinated. As a scratchy phonograph played "The Blue Danube," two of the girls swam a duet in time to the music. The production had been devised by Floyd Zimmerman, a young swimmer hired to give aquatic demonstrations at the Marine Theatre, which also had a small stage for style shows.[5]

Rose was inspired. "Do you see what I see?" he exclaimed to Dickey. "If it looks this good with two girls, imagine it with two hundred.... I'll build you a

Casa Mañana right on the Lake.... Picture it: Pavlova with water wings, Nijinsky in a bathing cap."[6] Despite the hyperbole, Dickey seemed interested and asked Rose what he would call this aquatic spectacle. Glancing around the shuttered midway, Rose's eyes fell on a penny arcade. "Watercade," he replied, "or, if you want to get fancy, Aquacade."[7]

The following day, Dickey arranged a meeting with the fair's executive committee. Rose outlined his plans for an aquatic spectacle staged in the manner of Casa Mañana, with hundreds of swimmers, divers, chorus people and a gigantic floating stage in place of the Marine Theatre's small barge. He also offered to present a version of the Pioneer Palace with its various old-time vaudeville acts. The committee accepted Rose's proposals and agreed to match his Fort Worth salary of $100,000. Rose returned to New York and had his production staff begin work on the idea. To assist with the strictly aquatic sequences, Rose hired Zimmerman and Aileen Riggin, another Olympic swimmer. Within a week, John Murray Anderson, Albert Johnson, and the others were on their way to Cleveland.

Rose's concept for a tremendous aquatic spectacular was hardly without precedent. The Romans had staged tremendous sea battles, called naumachiae, on a scale that dwarfed even Rose's grandiose conceptions. One such event, presented on a lake east of Rome in A.D. 52, involved 19,000 performers, many of whom fought to the death.[8] Nineteenth-century spectacle houses, such as Sadler's Wells in London, offered elaborate aquatic diversions, although these were more concerned with battles, waterfalls and other special effects than with elaborate swimming by large groups of performers. Niblo's Garden and other popular American theatres had often employed water tanks and aquatic sequences as part of their programs. In fact, the creation of spectacles, both aquatic and stagebound, had become a complex and refined part of American theatrical practice prior to 1900. Producers such as David Belasco, Augustin Daly and Steele MacKaye had achieved remarkable effects through the use of elaborate stage machinery and scrupulous attention to scenographic detail.

Ironically, the greatest of the New York spectacle houses, Thompson and Dundy's Hippodrome, once had a tremendous tank that had long since been covered over when Rose's *Jumbo* arrived. By this time, however, large indoor spectacle production had all but vanished from the theatrical scene. Even Rose, who had supposedly revived the genre with *Jumbo*, realized that live indoor spectacle could not hope to compete with motion pictures in terms of special effects.

Rose knew that the lavish productions he envisioned were only feasible outdoors. While this separated the *Aquacade* from much traditional stage spectacle, the show's reliance on elaborate mechanical effects and lighting placed it very much in the tradition of earlier open-air theatrical pageants (such as those produced by Percy MacKaye). The *Aquacade* was a unique hybrid of such disparate amusements as Parisian nightclubs, aquatic spectacles, vaudeville, historical pageants, and the Hollywood movie musicals of the day (exemplified by the work of Busby Berkeley).

But historical precedents mattered little to Rose. He saw the *Aquacade* as a gigantic nightclub show, clothed in the spectacular but wholesome setting of a P. T. Barnum circus. He felt that the show would make sophisticated cabaret diversions accessible to the general public while raising the lowbrow world of open-air amusements to the status of refined entertainment.

As he envisioned it, the *Aquacade* would combine the lavish production values and scale of *Jumbo* with the precision staging and elaborate mechanical effects of Casa Mañana. Rose saw it as the perfect expression of his style: sexy but not shameless, extravagant but not (in his view) vulgar. Rose wanted to use aquatics the way Ziegfeld had used fashion—as a way to show off the female form in an alluring but socially acceptable manner. While Ziegfeld sought to make risqué material high-toned and elegant, Rose wanted the girlie show to be a good-natured and wholesome part of the American entertainment tradition. And what could be more wholesomely erotic than hundreds of young healthy bodies in tight bathing suits?

Central to Rose's plans for the *Aquacade* was the engagement of star swimming talent. Olympic athletes were obviously needed, but to ensure a large audience Rose needed performers of national stature. He knew that Johnny Weissmuller—the former Olympic medal winner who had recently become famous as star of the successful *Tarzan* films—was easily the most popular and accomplished of America's male swimmers. To sign Weissmuller, however, Rose needed a female star of equal caliber, and that meant Eleanor Holm.

Holm had, by 1937, achieved a degree of notoriety rare among swimmers. She had won her first major title at fourteen and a year later placed fifth in the Olympic competition. She was a strikingly attractive girl whom the national magazines publicized as America's Olympic darling. At age sixteen, she had declined an offer from Florenz Ziegfeld to join the Follies. Unlike many young athletes, Holm was not the least bit shy and seemed to relish the publicity that surrounded her.

After winning her first Olympic medal in 1932, Holm moved to Hollywood and signed with Warner Brothers. Although she took acting lessons from Josephine Dillon (Clark Gable's first wife), Holm still thought of herself as a swimmer. In 1933 she married Arthur Jarrett, a well-known singer and orchestra leader whom she had met some years earlier. Although she continued under contract at Warner's and began singing in her husband's band, Holm already had her sights on the 1936 Olympics in Berlin.

Holm's Hollywood experiences and her tours with Jarrett's band brought out the more flamboyant aspects of her personality. She was particularly fond of regaling the press with such lines as, "I train on champagne and cigarettes."[9] At a time when America readily embraced colorful characters, Eleanor Holm was a big hit.

By the time the U.S. Olympic team left for Europe, her high-living reputation was common knowledge. Holm's vivacity endeared her to the public, but it cut no ice with Avery Brundage, head of the U.S. Olympic Committee. The strait-laced Brundage was a former hammer thrower who believed in rigid, teetotaling discipline. Needless to say, he took a dim view of Holm's penchant for publicity and champagne.

Soon after the team sailed for England aboard the S.S. *Manhattan,* Holm struck up a friendship with Charles MacArthur, who was accompanying his wife Helen Hayes to London. One evening Holm and MacArthur partook of a bit too much champagne. Holm had to be carried to her cabin, and MacArthur awoke the following morning to find his wife agitated, embarrassed and packing her trunks. Avery Brundage had dismissed Holm from the team for her spree with MacArthur. Hayes told her husband that she was getting off in Ireland to avoid the coming torrent of publicity.

There was indeed a considerable uproar. Ben Hecht later recalled that "The entire civilized world was set agog. Had the S.S. *Manhattan* hit an iceberg and gone down, she would have received no more newspaper space."[10] Even the normally prudish *New York Post* columnist Westbrook Pegler called Brundage and the Olympic Committee "a lot of male Aunt Hatties."[11] Holm was defiant and proclaimed innocently, "I've never made a secret of the fact that I like a good time."[12] Despite the general outcry and a petition signed by two-thirds of the U.S. team, Brundage stuck by his decision. Holm would not swim in Berlin.

Rose followed Holm's saga with great interest and once remarked to Richard Maney, "Some girl. She gets for nothing the press I have to pay a half dozen of you guys for."[13] Rose admired her fearless pursuit of the limelight, a drive he understood all too well. Her removal from the Olympic team had also touched a deeper chord. Rose could hardly forget that a drunken spree had cost him a championship seventeen years earlier. Although he was then deeply involved in the Fort Worth Centennial, Rose began to think of how to package Holm's unique talent for catching the public fancy.

Holm soon found that her well-publicized dismissal had created a wealth of opportunities. Movie contracts, swimming exhibitions, and other commercial offers appeared in rapid succession. It seemed that everyone was bidding for the services of the country's latest cause célèbre.

Never one to ignore a popular phenomenon, Rose contacted Holm's agent Lou Irwin and arranged a meeting. Rose was immediately taken by Holm's great beauty and supreme confidence. Holm was completely at ease in

Rose's imposing office and listened with casual indifference as he described the *Aquacade*. Her composure paid off. Rose had hoped to sign Holm for as little as $750 a week, but finally agreed to a contract paying $8000 a month plus benefits. The following week Rose engaged Johnny Weissmuller after some protracted negotiations with MGM, with whom the swimmer held an exclusive contract.[14] Rose also offered Holm's husband and his orchestra a job, but Jarrett refused, fearing that he would be upstaged by his wife's newfound notoriety. It was a decision he would soon regret.

Rose's initial fascination with Eleanor Holm soon blossomed into romance. Holm was wary of becoming involved with the husband of a famous and well-liked star, but admitted to finding Rose "fascinating... he has one of the most amazing minds I've ever seen."[15] His amazing bankroll probably helped, but there was little doubt that mutual chemistry was at work. Rose was clearly the more smitten of the two, and often sent Holm several telegrams a day when he was shuttling between Cleveland and Fort Worth. As the following excerpts indicate, Rose's flamboyance carried over into his love letters:

JUNE 8 FT. WORTH

SUGAR PLUM CANDY MOUTH AND THINGS THEY HANG ON CHRISTMAS TREES IF YOU THINK YOU'RE CONTENTED YOU OUGHT TO SEE ME **STOP** I FAIRLY OOZE HAPPINESS....

JUNE 19 FT.WORTH

MY DEAREST DARLING THIS IS A MAD HOUSE.... A TWELVE YEAR OLD KID WITH LIONS JUST CHECKED IN **STOP** A HUNCHBACK WHO WALKS A WIRE A HUNDRED FEET IN THE AIR WITHOUT A NET IS WAITING UPSTAIRS **STOP** FIVE SHOWS REHEARSING SIMULTANEOUSLY EACH IN SOME KIND OF TROUBLE BUT THROUGH THE SMOKE THAT SHINING FACE OF YOURS IS SMILING AT ME AND AS LONG AS YOU LOVE ME EVERYTHING'S OKAY
BILLY[16]

With the stars in place, *Aquacade* preparations began in earnest. While Johnson, duBois and Anderson completed their designs for the production, Rose held auditions for swimmers and divers in Florida and California. Rose, Zimmerman and Riggin saw thousands of performers before a cast of roughly two hundred swimmers, divers and aquatic stunt artists was assembled. Recalling the appeal of local talent in Fort Worth, Rose cast most of his chorus personnel in Cleveland.

As was the case in Fort Worth, Albert Johnson had no sooner finished his designs for the stage and theatre than construction began. In less than a month, 140 tons of steel, 300,000 feet of lumber and 40,000 square feet of

Figure 15. *Aquacade* Amphitheatre, Great Lakes Exposition, 1937
(Courtesy Billy Rose Theatre Collection, New York Public Library, Astor, Lenox and Tilden Foundations)

corrugated iron came together to create a 7000-seat amphitheatre on the shores of Lake Erie (fig. 15). Two 65-foot diving towers framed a 130-foot by 80-foot stage that rested on two huge barges. Similar in many respects to the Casa Mañana stage, the platform could move back and forth over the water while its center section revolved. The stage was constructed in a Cleveland shipyard and towed to the fair site by six tugboats.[17] The configuration of the auditorium also resembled Casa Mañana, with 2000 tables in the front section for dinner customers and an additional 3000 seats for those wishing only to see the show.

While *Aquacade* construction proceeded, Rose oversaw the creation of a Pioneer Palace even larger than the Fort Worth original. The bar in the Cleveland version (which also served as the stage) was one hundred feet long and was equipped with a mechanical forestage that extended from beneath the bar. Rose employed many of the same artists featured in Fort Worth as well as several additional acts. One of the more notable new routines was Heavenly Hooves, a pair of Shetland ponies that tap danced on the bar.

70 Cleveland, 1937: The First Aquacade

When *Aquacade* rehearsals began in early March, it was still too cold in Cleveland for outdoor swimming. Since no indoor pool could accommodate the formations that Anderson and Zimmerman devised, rehearsals took place in a hotel ballroom. The two men would work out the geometric patterns of the routines and have the resulting designs painted on the floor. Zimmerman then instructed the swimmers in the appropriate strokes and ran through each sequence with music until the timing was right. Surprisingly, this method proved remarkably effective. Few adjustments were necessary once the cast took to the water.[18]

Carlton Winckler, who had performed miracles with the technical arrangements at Fort Worth, outdid himself at Cleveland. The extreme depth of the stage and house, coupled with the floating platform's need to advance and recede nearly one hundred feet, placed unusual demands on the lighting. To ensure proper illumination of the stage, instruments had to be devised with an effective throw of nearly four hundred feet. Winckler had lighting engineers create 240 special lenses and forty portable spotlights in addition to the hundreds of regular lights required for the show.

He also constructed a water curtain that rose forty feet from a row of two hundred nozzles in front of the stage. Lights from various points in the auditorium were angled to create colorful patterns on the mist. To orchestrate the various effects, Winckler set up a system of twelve control boards and communicated with each operator from a central console.[19]

Winckler and Anderson had also planned elaborate underwater lighting effects, but abandoned them when the submerged lamps revealed an excess of garbage on the shallow lakebed. The trash problem was aggravated once the floating stage was in place, for its movements often brought bizarre flotsam and jetsam to the surface. In the middle of one dress rehearsal, a dead cow bobbed up among the swimmers.[20]

The *Aquacade* script was pieced together from the two Casa Mañana revues. Instead of world's fairs, the scenes were placed at various famous American beaches, such as Coney Island and Miami. The *Aquacade* finale was derived from the "It Can't Happen Here" sequence planned for the 1937 Casa Mañana revue.[21] Most of the music was new, although Dana Suesse's score had to accommodate a few turn-of-the-century standards. As with Casa Mañana, two bands were placed on opposite sides of the stage, in this case under the diving towers. Albert Johnson's settings included a series of screens and panels that were turned and shifted to provide changes in color and decor.

Publicity was hardly as flamboyant as Ned Alvord's in Fort Worth, although Richard Maney did come up with an amusing bit of puffery that described the show as employing "Lake Erie for a swimming pool and Canada as the backdrop." This slogan tended to ignore the fact that, even with binoculars, the shoreline of Canada was miles removed from view. Never one to forget a successful pitch, Rose again ran the "What Is It?" style of advertisements he had used years earlier with Casino de Paree (fig. 16).

To justify the show's billing as novel entertainment, Rose decided on new labels for his performers. They were called, depending on their role and gender: Aquabelles, Aquabeaux, Aquafemmes, Aquaclowns, Aquadolls, Aquadudes, Aquagals and Aquasteppers. In keeping with another long-standing Rose tradition, the *Aquacade* was also a relative bargain, considering its tremendous production costs. There were three shows daily with prices ranging from $1.00 for general admission to $3.50 for dinner and the show. Dancing was offered during intermission with music provided by a resident orchestra and a visiting big-name band.

When the *Aquacade* opened on May 29, 1937, the rain that plagued dress rehearsals lifted, and clear skies prevailed at curtain time. The show began with the two orchestras trading fanfares and then uniting for a final flourish as announcer Bob Lawrence introduced the first scene, "A Beach in California." The great stage floated away from the audience as a swimsuited chorus of Aquadolls entered with The Eight Men of Manhattan to sing "We Rule the Waves":

>We rule the waves, the permanent waves
>Our brotherhood saves the lives of wives
>Resigned to gloom....
>We leisurely soak up scotch and watch
>The breakers boom.
>We haven't yet been wet, although we follow the She,
>Eight handsome sons, sons of a beach resort are we![22]

Eleanor Holm then made her entrance in a full-length mink, which fell casually to reveal a shimmering silver swimsuit. As she swam the length of the pool, Bob Lawrence sang a song reminding the audience of her checkered past:

>Just a glass of wine and you were ruled off,
>Off the U.S.A. Olympic team,
>But my love for you has never cooled off,
>And today's the birthday of a dream...[23]

Holm's introduction was followed by the first big precision swimming routine. Two hundred swimmers and a dozen divers executed their intricate maneuvers to the accompaniment of live music. The complex formations bore a remarkable resemblance to the motion picture sequences choreographed by

WHAT IS IT?

IS IT A FASHION SHOW? No! Though it presents the last word in modern and period clothes, designed by RAOUL PENE DuBOIS, featuring the "Dress of the Stars" (500 yards of spangle-embroidered satin).

IS IT A GIRL SHOW? No! Though it presents—artistically to be sure—500 of the most glamorous Aquafemmes on which the eyes have ever feasted.

IS IT A THEATRE? No! Though it presents a cast of world-famous stage personalities, directed by JOHN MURRAY ANDERSON, on the largest stage in the world.

IS IT A WATER SHOW? No! Though it stars JOHNNY (TARZAN) WEISSMULLER, ELEANOR HOLM JARRETT — DICK DEGENER and MARSHALL WAYNE 1936 Olympic Champions, and 100 (count 'em) beautiful Aquabelles.

IS IT A RESTAURANT? No! Though you can dine sumptuously (and reasonably), table d' hote or a la carte, with the cuisine directed by an internationally-known chef.

IS IT A NIGHT CLUB? No! Though you may dance under the stars, on a fabulous floating stage, to the music of America's best-known orchestras.

IS IT AN OPERETTA? No! Though is has an original score of music, especially composed by DANA SUESS, presented against startling settings designed by ALBERT JOHNSON.

IS IT A MUSICAL COMEDY? No! Though its enormous dancing chorus is staged by Broadway's ace dance director, ROBERT ALTON, and features the madcap antics of America's outstanding water clown, STUBBY KREUGER, plus a host of stage headliners.

WHAT IS IT? Billy Rose's AQUACADE—the newest thing in American entertainment—a $10 show scaled down to fit the purse of the times. You'll tell your grandchildren about it some day.

Broadway at Lake Erie

Figure 16. Advertisement for Cleveland *Aquacade*, 1937
(Courtesy Billy Rose Theatre Collection, New York Public Library, Astor, Lenox and Tilden Foundations)

Cleveland, 1937: The First Aquacade 73

Figure 17. Scene from Cleveland *Aquacade*, 1937
(Courtesy Billy Rose Theatre Collection, New York Public Library, Astor, Lenox and Tilden Foundations)

Busby Berkeley for overhead cameras (fig. 17). These aquatic performances made a vivid impression on those who saw them: "You just can't imagine how graceful it looked.... The entire show was just so silky and precise... the swimmers moved so easily through the water. I don't know how they managed to time it that perfectly with the music... it was like ballet, only smoother.... I kept thinking of swans."[24]

The surviving photographs and newsreel footage of the various Aquacades, while hardly an adequate measure of their visual impact, do convey some of the remarkable precision and grace the swimmers achieved. Their accomplishments were all the more impressive in light of the limited rehearsal time spent in the water. Owing to bad weather and last-minute modifications to the stage, Anderson and Zimmerman had barely a week to work on their numbers in the lake.[25]

After the last swimmer had paddled from view beneath the diving platforms, Robert Alton closed the first scene with one of his more amusing choreographic conceits, the self-partnering chorus. In a clever sleight-of-hand combination of costuming and staging, the chorus was attired in costumes divided down the middle into half tuxedos and half evening gowns. The performer had only to hold her right hand aloft with her left to give the impression of a couple dancing. The number was appropriately entitled "Half and Half" (fig. 18).[26]

The second scene, "Coney Island, 1905," began with a medley of such period standards as "Good Old Summer Time" and "By the Beautiful Sea." Following a Gibson-girl costume parade and a stage-filling bicycle routine, the trademark Tarzan yell introduced Johnny Weissmuller. After a quick demonstration of his swimming prowess, Weissmuller and Aquaclown Stubby Krueger finished the scene with a series of comic dives by Krueger, who managed to run, bounce, and fall off five different diving boards.

A particularly intriguing effect came after intermission when the stage and pool lights were turned off and the chorus swam by in luminous bathing suits, caps and gloves. They were followed by boats with glowing sails and a stage chorus waving large luminous feathers. As the Frazee Sisters sang "Strangers in the Dark," Holm and Weissmuller, also attired in glowing swimwear, performed their only duet of the show. The sight of the two Olympians racing through the darkened pool was one of the most compelling in the show.[27]

The *Aquacade* concluded with the opulent tableaux of "It Can't Happen Here." This version elaborated on the isolationist sentiments of its predecessor with such additional lyrics as "Let no Red try to spread/chaos where we now have liberty."[28] As at Casa Mañana, this scene relied heavily on costumes and resplendent scenography.

Another sequence borrowed from Fort Worth involved Miss Liberty, who ascended a wide row of steps center-stage, followed by attendants manipulating her five-hundred yard train of rhinestone-covered satin. Upon reaching the top of the platform, she rose an additional hundred feet on an elevator while a chorus of Aquafemmes in white patent leather costumes walked down the steps carrying sheaves of wheat and tridents to symbolize the nation's resources on land and sea.

At the top of her elevator ride, Miss Liberty struck a heroic pose and saluted, signaling explosions of fireworks from around the amphitheatre. The finale featured a fleet of model battleships (each roughly twenty feet in length) cruising in front of the stage while the entire cast of three hundred took their bows (fig. 19).[29]

Rose's marine circus was everything Dickey and the exposition's backers hoped it would be. Sellout crowds were frequent, due in no small measure to the producer's front-page courtship of Eleanor Holm. As a result of substantial profits from the Pioneer Palace and a rain-free summer, Cleveland managed to recoup most of its first-season losses.

Figure 18. "Half and Half," Number from Cleveland *Aquacade*, 1937 *(Courtesy Billy Rose Theatre Collection, New York Public Library, Astor, Lenox and Tilden Foundations)*

76   Cleveland, 1937: The First Aquacade

Figure 19. Finale of Cleveland *Aquacade*, 1937
(Courtesy Billy Rose Theatre Collection, New York Public Library, Astor, Lenox and Tilden Foundations)

The press hailed the *Aquacade* as a startling new form of spectacle. "For everything was so new and strange, so exciting and so splendidly sensuous," wrote one reviewer, "that it became of its kind quite the finest show on earth."[30] Rose was being called the greatest innovator in the history of popular amusement, and few people disputed it. In point of fact, Rose rarely did anything completely new; he merely added to and refined the same material. The *Aquacade* was a logical extension of Casa Mañana, which had evolved from Casino de Paree and *Jumbo,* which sprang from *Crazy Quilt,* which in turn grew out of *Sweet and Low,* and so on. Beginning with the Backstage Club in 1925, Rose brought forward from one enterprise to the next those features that were most popular. Critics who had followed his work for ten years simply ignored this. Their lapse of memory was surprising, but understandable.

By now Rose had developed an aura of invincibility as a producer of spectacular entertainments. His ballyhoo had become an integral part of the shows themselves, serving both to whet the public appetite and create a smoke screen around the actual event. Thanks to the prodigious efforts of his press agents, Rose's habit of dressing up recycled acts was obscured by the image of a colorful little underdog who always did the impossible on a grand scale.

His careful cultivation of this persona was also part of a more private goal. Ever since plans were announced for a 1939 New York World's Fair, Rose assumed that he would play a prominent role in the development of its entertainments. Since he hoped to secure a divorce from Fanny Brice and marry Eleanor Holm, a lucrative concession at the New York World's Fair was vital for the sort of life he envisioned with his bride-to-be.

Soon after the Cleveland Exposition closed, Rose leased the French Casino nightclub on Broadway and promptly announced his intention to produce an indoor version of Casa Mañana. Rose hoped that revenue from the club would provide the capital he needed for a truly gargantuan production at the 1939 fair.

Before work on his new project could begin, however, Rose received some unexpected and disturbing news: New York World's Fair boss Grover Whalen had appointed a man named John Krimsky to be director of entertainment. Krimsky, the son-in-law of a Tammany contractor, had almost no show business experience. His only previous credit was producing a nineteenth-century melodrama in the basement of a former church. Rose was crushed. He was unable to imagine a world's fair in New York that did not include him.

As he often did when things seemed bleak, Rose sought the advice of Bernard Baruch. Baruch calmly suggested that he forget the fair, as Whalen had obviously made his decision. Despite this counsel, Rose was determined to prevail. "My private crystal ball told me the New York World's Fair was the pot of gold at the end of my rainbow," he later wrote. "No matter what the odds were, I had to get a crack at it."[31]

6
Nightclubs, 1938–1951

In the fall of 1937, Rose's appetite for publicity began to wane. The indiscreet courtship of Eleanor Holm led to his being branded "Public Heel Number 1" by the national columnists. "Billy Rose may have the nation's headlines," wrote Walter Winchell, "but Fanny Brice has its heart."[1] Normally immune to such barbs, Rose became exceedingly camera shy. He was now aware that one could not suddenly quit the limelight after actively seeking it for fifteen years. But more important, he realized that the scandal could ruin his chances at the New York World's Fair.

The situation was further aggravated when Rose decided to produce a touring show after the Cleveland *Aquacade* closed. Entitled *Show of Shows*, it was an ill-conceived hodgepodge assembled by a production team that had worked continuously for eighteen months. The show featured hastily rehearsed segments from the Fort Worth and Cleveland fairs, as well as numbers from *Crazy Quilt,* Casino de Paree and *Jumbo*. Although poorly prepared and under financed, *Show of Shows* managed to tour the West for nearly three months.

Rose's problems began when he decided to accompany the tour, for which Eleanor Holm was a principal star. Holm and Rose, who had little experience avoiding reporters, were soon photographed arm and arm in a succession of hotel lobbies. Speculation was fanned by Rose's offhand remarks to reporters in Denver, where he said of Fanny Brice, "It's no fun being married to an electric light."[2]

For her part, Brice maintained a more dignified public veneer. She was not, however, above an occasional private dig. Several days after Rose's comments in Denver, she called his hotel room in the middle of the night. "Bill, this is Fanny," she announced. "There's something I've been meaning to ask you. Is aquacade one word or two?"[3]

Stormy public and private relations notwithstanding, Rose pressed ahead with his plans for the New York World's Fair. Although dismayed by John Krimsky's appointment as director of entertainment, Rose felt that he could still obtain an amusement concession. He met with Krimsky only to be informed that the fair had all the amusements it needed. When Rose inquired about the nature of the attractions, he was shown flyers for wax shows and a brochure describing a model of the Holy Land with moving miniature figures. There was a strong man named Peter the Great who lifted a table into the air with his teeth while a girl did a tap dance routine on it. Krimsky was also negotiating with a horseshoe tosser who could "set off torpedoes, light matches and slice apples in half."[4] He was particularly excited by an attraction which claimed to display "the genuine body, flesh and bones of John Wilkes Booth."[5]

When Rose pointed out that side-show acts might not be appropriate for the New York World's Fair, Krimsky produced pages of figures demonstrating the drawing power of his attractions. The noble and sophisticated enterprise envisioned by the fair's president Grover Whalen had somehow failed to register with John Krimsky. Rose was discouraged, but still determined.

After his meeting with Krimsky, Rose approached Earl Andrews, the manager of New York State's concession at the fair, for which a large amphitheatre was being constructed. Andrews told him that the fair was negotiating with the Shuberts, who had offered to produce an operetta and guarantee the fair twenty percent of the gross. Rose knew such an offer was impossible and told Andrews, "If J. J. Shubert gives you 20% of his gross, I'll put on a cap and take tickets."[6] Frustrated by conventional channels, Rose decided to take his case directly to Grover Whalen.

Grover Aloysius Whalen was a tall, dapper man whose trademark lapel flower earned him the nickname "Gardenia of the Law" while he was New York's police commissioner. Born on President Cleveland's wedding day (hence the name Grover), Whalen began his career in politics under Mayor John Hylan in 1917. His patrician features and preference for formal dress made him a great success at city functions. For many years he greeted famous visitors, presided over parades, and otherwise presented his refined and elegant visage at civic events. In between public assignments, Whalen operated a lucrative business as a merchandising consultant with such clients as John Wannamaker, the IRT subway system and Coty Perfumes.[7]

Whalen was chairman of the board of Schenley Products, a major distiller of spirits, when he resigned in 1935 to plan and promote the New York World's Fair. By the fall of 1937, Whalen was busy overseeing the completion of the Flushing Meadow fair site and attending to countless other details of the $157-million project.[8] The last thing on his mind was whether or not Billy Rose had a concession in the amusement zone.

After failing to get past Whalen's secretary, Rose called New York state senator John Dunnigan (chairman of the the state world's fair committee), who arranged a meeting with the fair's executive committee. To impress

Whalen and the other officials, Rose prepared a short film of his fair productions, which included newsreel footage of the Cleveland and Fort Worth Fairs and material from an MGM two-reeler about Casa Mañana.

Despite Rose's typically persuasive presentation, Whalen and the committee were unimpressed and politely offered to give his requests due consideration. But most of the officials believed that the fair could survive on its merits as a cultural event without the benefit of elaborate theatrical entertainments. Rose's argument for big cash flow amusements fell on deaf ears. A more subtle approach would be required to get his point across.

From what he knew of Whalen's history and personality, Rose thought that he could appeal to the fair president's vanity. There was little doubt that Whalen relished the limelight. He had organized New York's mammoth National Recovery Administration and Lindbergh parades, two of the city's biggest civic pageants. Rose saw an opportunity in Whalen's weakness for lavish events, and he decided to exploit it.

Soon after his unsuccessful presentation before the fair committee, Rose hit upon an idea that played directly on Whalen's penchant for being at the center of things. Although he had already begun renovating Fred Fischer's old French Casino, Rose still had not settled on a show to open the New York Casa Mañana. After discussions with John Murray Anderson, Rose decided to make Whalen and the fair the subjects of a revue, to which he gave the suitably coy title *Let's Play Fair*. Since the show was supposed to secure Rose a job, he cast Oscar Shaw, one of Hollywood's more dashing matinee idols, as Whalen.

Anderson and Rose had by now become remarkably proficient at creating revues and managed to script *Let's Play Fair* completely in less than two weeks. They began by establishing a general theme, in this case the search for talent to fill the fair's amusement section. The show was then broken down into production numbers and specialty acts that could be pieced together loosely around the theme. Once specific acts had been signed, Rose wrote the script and Dana Suesse began work on the music. Despite its loose construction, *Let's Play Fair* was unusual for a nightclub revue in having both a book and a specially written score.

Rose's claims to the contrary, the New York Casa Mañana was far more akin to Casino de Paree and the Billy Rose Music Hall than to the expansive open-air Fort Worth show. The stage and audience arrangements were similar to those in his earlier clubs, albeit with the potential for more elaborate technical effects. Rose installed a retractable thrust stage and a revolve that could elevate and move forward while turning. Another unique facility was the Palm Beach Bar (fig. 20), which featured private cabanas with sunlamps and attendants to offer patrons, in the words of a brochure, "Vitamin D with swing music."[9]

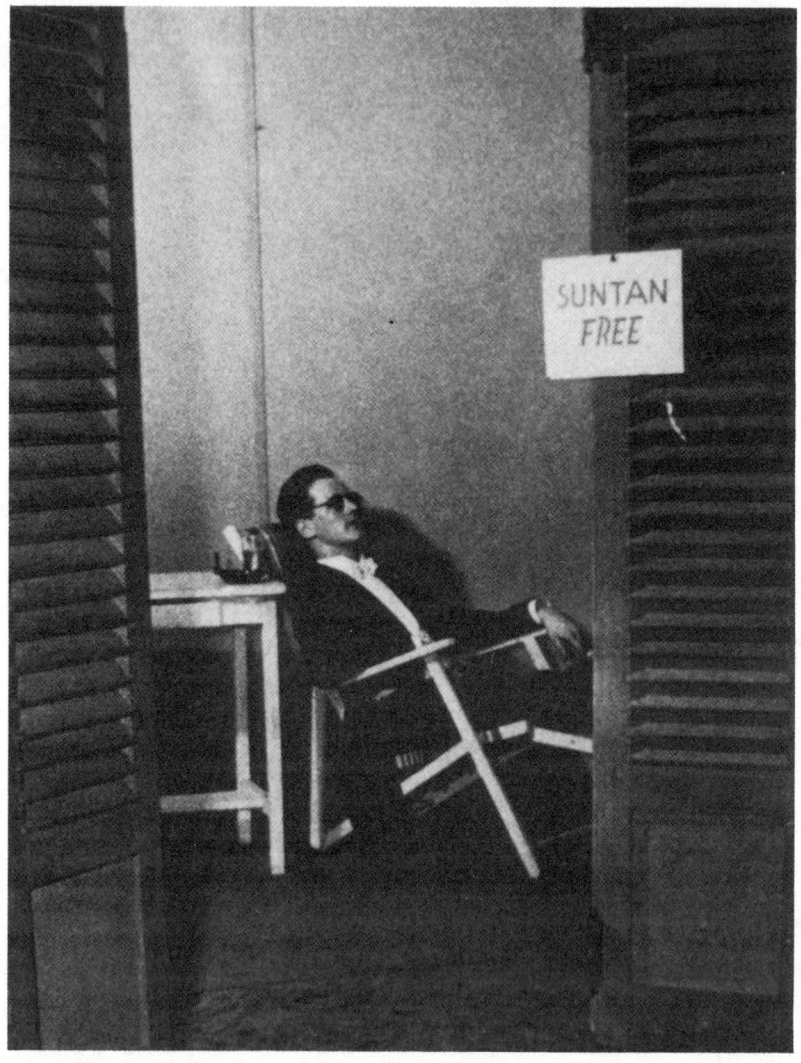

Figure 20. Palm Beach Bar, Casa Mañana, New York, 1938
(Courtesy Billy Rose Theatre Collection, New York Public Library, Astor, Lenox and Tilden Foundations)

In addition to Oscar Shaw, Rose assembled a stellar cast that included Sally Rand, Morton Downey, Tom Patricola and the popular comedian Doc Rockwell. The Tiny Rosebuds (Rose's plump ballerinas) were rechristened The Elsa Maxwell Girls in honor of New York's foremost giver of dinner parties. Other specialty acts included five trained Bengal tigers, the comedy team of Willie, West and McGinty, and a nude contortionist dancer named Hinda Wassau.

Since Rose had been absent from the New York theatre scene for nearly two years, there was considerable interest in the nature of his new project. Rose carefully orchestrated the publicity by leaking bits and pieces of the script to the press at regular intervals. He also composed a breezy advertisement that set forth his ideas on how a nightclub should be run:

PLAIN TALK

I'M NOT SURE that I know what people like in a nightclub, but I think I do know what they DON'T like. With a few exceptions, the Broadway password has always been, "NEVER GIVE A SUCKER AN EVEN BREAK." I DON'T LIKE IT. I don't think a front table is worth a $5.00 tip. I resent being told I can't understand the show without a program.... I don't like thumbs in my coffee... and I resent having gardenias shoved down my throat. ETC! ETC! ETC![10]

The advertisement went on to state that Rose's new club was dedicated to the interests of "Mr. Forgotten Man (the guy who pays the check)."[11] Although admission was $10 for the premiere, regular prices were generally lower than most competing nightclubs, with a basic dinner minimum of $2.50 and no cover charge. To avoid the poor management that plagued his earlier clubs, Rose hired Richard Daley, an experienced hotel executive, to oversee daily operations and food service at Casa Mañana.

Rose promised that although most New York clubs had changed little since the days of burlesque, his girlie shows would be refreshing and novel. In this case the novelty consisted of several dozen tall showgirls from Fort Worth, including six-foot-two-inch Mary Dowell. "I glorify wholesomeness," Rose said in stating his theory of nightclub shows. "I often pass up a pretty girl because she looks a little blasé. I like girls to whom the theatre is still a novelty, still exciting."[12]

Rose spent lavishly to impress Whalen, and invested more than $100,000 of his own money in a show that ran less than two hours. Much of the expense centered on the costumes, which were opulent even by Raoul Pène duBois's standards. Oscar Shaw's impeccably tailored morning coat and striped trousers cost $300 and were specially sewn by an English tailor who had made suits for Whalen. There were the usual diaphanous chorus gowns and a dress with an eighty-five-foot train that required forty-eight people to manipulate.

The dress was constructed from five hundred yards of satin and took a dozen costumers two weeks to sew.

All of Rose's elaborate preparations would have gone for naught had his audience of one chosen to ignore it. Whalen, however, took the bait immediately after the show was announced. "An hour after the morning papers hit the street," Rose recalled, "Mr. Whalen was on the phone to ask if I was going to ridicule him. I knew that no man could be disinterested in a show about himself."[13] Two weeks before *Let's Play Fair* opened, Rose sent Whalen a telegram that read: "Dear Grover, I'm saving a down-front table for you and your party on opening night. Come and see yourself as others see you. Kind regards, Billy."[14] Whalen and his guests arrived at the theatre thirty minutes before curtain time.

On January 18, 1938, 1100 celebrities, critics and society denizens joined Whalen for the opening of *Let's Play Fair,* which now bore the subtitle, "A Revusical Comedy."[15] The show opened in the offices of the New York World's Fair with a beaming Whalen (Oscar Shaw with moustache and gardenia) announcing the upcoming fair in song:

> It must be terrific'ly scientific in scope.
> It must be modernistic and yet artistic, I hope.
> Let's reproduce Gibraltar in cellophane
> And the Eiffel Tower in soap....[16]

Shaw had barely finished his song when Doc Rockwell entered and introduced himself as a "Professor of Anatomy." Rockwell told Shaw that the key to a successful fair was beautiful women and lots of them. Recalling Sally Rand and the 1933 Chicago Fair, Rockwell remarked, "Without her hips it would have been a bust."[17]

When Shaw replied that he had seen the Century of Progress Exposition but missed Rand's performance, Rockwell countered, "That's like seeing the horse and missing Lady Godiva." He then asked the audience if they would like to see Rand "in the flesh," and received tumultuous applause. "Ah, the thighs have it," he exclaimed, "Miss Sally Rand!" Rand then did a variation on her famous fan dance that substituted a model of the fair's Perisphere for the usual feathers (fig. 21). Rockwell observed that "Here we have a bit of astronomy, showing that when a globe passes in front of a heavenly body, we have an eclipse of the moon."[18]

Shaw's Whalen was favorably impressed and sent Rockwell around the world to gather suitable talent for the fair. His departure led to the show's first big dance sequence, with Shaw singing "Throw a Little Party." The song set forth some of Rose's notions about the proper character of a world's fair:

Figure 21. Sally Rand and Oscar Shaw in *Let's Play Fair*, 1938
(Courtesy Billy Rose Theatre Collection, New York Public Library, Astor, Lenox and Tilden Foundations)

> Spend a hundred million
> And make it gay,
> Top Chicago
> Top Broadway.
> Ford and General Motors
> Won't attract the floaters
> Whoopee and machinery don't blend.
> Sign up Sally Rand
> And watch the masses unbend....
> Nothing very arty,
> Cohen and McCarty
> Want to let down their hair.
> Throw a little party
> In every part of the Fair[19]

The show provided several other opportunities for Rose to expound lyrically on his theories of mass entertainment. The most outrageous of these occurred at the beginning of the second act when Shaw touched on the subject of merchandising the exposition. The Frazee Sisters then revealed Rose's promotional approach in a song entitled, "Give Them Girls":

> You can sell your Quaker Oats if you give them girls.
> You can sell the soap that floats if you give them
>   girls.
> Motor boats or motor cars
> Crackerjack or Hershey bars
> Your sales will spurt with every skirt
> Who rolls her eyes instead of her r's....
> They'll eat your Wheaties if you give 'em sweeties.
> They'll buy Gillettes and Gems if you give 'em fems....
> Wrap your Jello in brassieres and you'll have seven
>   banner years.
> Females!
> Cash Sales!
> Feed them Sex with a capital "X"
> You can sell them coal in hell if you give them girls.[20]

Raoul Pène duBois, who designed the settings as well as the costumes, achieved a number of startling scenic effects. There was a version of the Shangri-la scene from Fort Worth which employed cellophane, mirrors, elevators and a revolve. The *New York Herald Tribune*'s reviewer described the scene, "in which a crystal temple only faintly hid the members of the chorus in scanty costumes as a revolving stage spun and moved forward at the same time."[21] Another amusing scenic effect was the "Glass Woman," a novel mannequin constructed by Doc Rockwell. The voluptuous contraption was designed to light up in appropriate places to accompany his ribald lecture on female anatomy.[22]

After additional appearances by the stars and specialty acts, the revue closed with Shaw's dashing Grover Whalen singing the finale, "New York on Parade":

> Drink a toast from coast to coast
> To the most colossal fair on earth.
> We've outdone everyone, not forgetting
>   Paris and Fort Worth....
> At last our splendor will be displayed
> By Henry Ford and Penny Arcade.
> Swing wide the gate—congratulate
> New York on parade![23]

The show's congratulatory tone had its desired effect on Whalen, who was in a glowing mood after an evening of complimentary champagne. Before leaving the club, he invited Rose to come to his office the following day to discuss the fair. An agreement was soon reached which called for Rose to present a production in the New York State Amphitheatre, the nature and title of which were left undetermined. Rose guaranteed the fair ten percent of the gross in exchange for the promise that there would be no other show on the grounds playing to more than 1500 persons. Although the contractual arrangements had been quickly concluded, it would be several months before Rose finally decided on a production for the fair.[24]

Let's Play Fair was well received by the press and soon played to capacity houses. Despite the show's success, Rose decided to close it in April and switch to a less elaborate program of vaudeville and variety acts, partly out of a desire to reduce the club's substantial overhead. Although the format was less novel, the quality of the entertainment remained high. Rose's *Streamlined Varieties* featured a changing cast of headliners including Bud Abbott and Lou Costello, Helen Morgan, the Three Stooges, Jack Benny, and Lou Holtz. Betty Hutton got her start in these programs as did Ethel Waters, who appeared at Casa Mañana before her Broadway stage debut in *Mamba's Daughters*. Other newcomers included Danny Kaye, Vera-Ellen and Van Johnson, who made one of his first New York appearances in the Casa Mañana chorus.

Although Casa Mañana's bill was thoroughly star-studded, there was considerable doubt as to the continued appeal of vaudeville-style programs, even in so posh a setting. Some questioned whether *Streamlined Varieties* even rated consideration as a vaudeville show. "This is not the close-knit and gaudy vaudeville... of performers terrified that thirty seconds of their ten minutes might turn out to be boring," wrote Brooks Atkinson. "An eating house is no place for vaudeville... it is on the formal side... stiff and detached from merriment. Evening clothes are the harness of the gentry; they are the death of gusty performing."[25] Atkinson's comments cut to the heart of the problem. *Streamlined Varieties* was out of place in a club that styled itself as sophisticated and contemporary. More important, vaudeville itself was dying out and no longer constituted a vital force in popular theatre.

Sensing that he might be out of step with the times, Rose wrote a column for the *New York Post* that began, "As far as I am concerned, vaudeville is as dead as Kelcey's ancestors."[26] He noted that motion pictures and radio had all but eliminated the national audience for vaudeville, despite the continued popularity of variety acts in nightclubs. Rose also observed that the structure of the theatrical booking business made a resurgence of the vaudeville circuit highly unlikely. Shortly after this pronouncement, however, Rose embarked on a project that completely ignored his published assertions.

In early October of 1938, two men came to Rose with a proposal. James Lee, an investment banker, and Charles Ornstein, manager of the Hotel Paramount, were interested in reviving the fortunes of that decaying hotel. Once a respectable establishment, the Paramount was now a flophouse for transients and prostitutes. Lee and Ornstein wanted Rose to open a nightclub in the hotel's basement in hopes that it would improve the property's image and value. Although its location (Forty-sixth Street between Eighth Avenue and Broadway) was less than ideal, Rose agreed to take a look at the space.

Formerly the hotel's grill, the basement had been unused for many years. It was a moldy rat-infested cavern that John Murray Anderson later described as "a place the Count of Monte Cristo might have been glad to dig himself out of."[27] Sensing Rose's reservations about the project, Ornstein offered to modify the premises to his specifications for a flat yearly rental of only $15,000. Rose took another look around at the crumbling plaster walls and agreed to the terms on the spot. As soon as the lease was signed, Rose and Anderson announced chorus auditions and Albert Johnson began work on the interior.

Whereas Casa Mañana had attempted to be chic and up-to-date, Rose envisioned the new club as a variation on the Pioneer Palace's Gay Nineties-style decor and attractions. He reasoned that many of the variety acts that seemed out of place in Casa Mañana's elegant surroundings would be right at home in a saloon. The fact that the club was in a basement also suggested a less refined atmosphere.

In many respects the new venture was a logical extension of Rose's earlier use of nostalgia in his revues, clubs and fair productions.[28] Old-time entertainment was not only popular but cost-effective. The aging vaudeville acts, retired stars and carnival performers that Rose favored could be hired at a fraction of the salary of major contemporary stars. In addition, the trouble and expense of composing or paying royalties on new songs could be virtually eliminated. A nostalgic cabaret also had a great appeal to tourists and older customers who were put off by overly sophisticated nightclub shows.

To realize Rose's Gay Nineties concept, Albert Johnson designed an ornate red interior trimmed in blue and white that rivaled even his opulent Hippodrome renovations. The club seated seven hundred at tables arranged around a bar stage similar to the one at the Pioneer Palace. Rose had wanted to call the place the Silver Dollar, but Anderson felt the lavish interior demanded a more elegant name. They settled on the Diamond Horseshoe, an allusion to the Metropolitan Opera's tier of exclusive boxes.

If one accepts Fred Allen's definition of a nightclub as "an upholstered sewer," then the Diamond Horseshoe was certainly among the most sumptuous sewers ever constructed. The club's blazing red color scheme and rococo appointments exceeded even the most florid period caricature (fig. 22). Its antique beveled mirrors, crystal chandeliers and ornate bar called to mind nothing so much as a Walt Disney treatment of Luchow's. As with his other entertainments, Rose had a theory about saloons. "A nightclub must be

Figure 22. Interior of the Diamond Horseshoe, ca. 1940
(Courtesy Billy Rose Theatre Collection, New York Public Library, Astor, Lenox and Tilden Foundations)

predominantly red. Most of the great cafés of the world are painted bright red," he declared. "Also a nightclub must not be too comfortable. People get a thrill out of being crowded together... some infectious gaiety makes them start laughing."[29]

Throughout October and November Johnson, Anderson and Rose worked feverishly to prepare the club for opening by the first of the year. Johnson and Anderson managed to acquire old saloon fittings including brass bar rails, mirrors and gilded wall sconces. The performers selected for the club were in perfect keeping with its decor. In addition to many of Rose's favorites, such as Lulu Bates, Tom Patricola, Eddie Leonard and Ann Pennington, Anderson engaged Gilda Gray, Mae Murray, Harriet Hoctor and Fritzi Scheff.

The first production was based on a typical evening in the lives of Diamond Jim Brady and Lillian Russell, with scenes set at such period landmarks as Rector's and Delmonico's. To create the proper atmosphere,

Rose decorated the lobby and stairwells with reproductions of Brady's prodigious jewelry collection. He hired a barbershop quartet to perform between shows.

Fittingly titled *The Turn of the Century*, the premiere Diamond Horseshoe production opened on Christmas Day, 1938. Fritzi Scheff appeared in a $20,000 fur cloak to sing "Kiss Me Again," which she had first performed at the opening of Victor Herbert's *Mademoiselle Modiste* thirty-three years earlier to the day.[30] Her first entrance precipitated a three-minute standing ovation.[31]

The proceedings also came to a halt when Harry Armstrong (who wrote "Sweet Adeline") and Joe Howard (author of "I Wonder Who's Kissing Her Now") appeared to lead the audience in a medley of old-time favorites. To ensure spirited participation, lyric sheets were placed on each table with instructions printed in bold red type: "IF YOU CAN'T SING GOOD, SING LOUD."[32] Rose saw the music as essential to the club's success. "They get happier faster to old songs," he observed. "You can feel the joy of recognition as the audience recalls an old song."[33]

Following the sing-along, Lulu Bates sang the wonderfully overwrought ballad, "A Bird in a Gilded Cage," while Eddie Eddy the cry artist played a cello and wept into a bucket. The Tiny Rosebuds performed a burlesque routine which they closed by tossing their waistband-size garter belts into the audience. Eddie Leonard, one of the last great minstrels, also appeared, as did a relative newcomer named Beatrice Kay, who had made her childhood debut in Murray Anderson's 1920 production of *What's in a Name?*[34]

The press immediately christened the Diamond Horseshoe a sensation. The glowing reviews and a host of national magazine articles on the club kept *The Turn of the Century* running seventeen months. The production, which cost $33,000 to open, grossed $982,000 in its first twelve months. The show established a pattern for the Diamond Horseshoe, with most productions running ten to twelve months each, and some nearly two years.

For Rose the formula was simple, although it took him thirteen years to perfect it. The main ingredients were low prices, an exciting pace, familiar old-time material, and an overall feeling of continuous festivity. "I am a great believer in fanfares," he once said. "We never start with a medley or an overture.... During the show, we have a total of fifteen fanfares.... It's strictly a trip hammer technique. A fanfare says, 'Lay down your knife and fork, the Indians are coming.'"[35]

Rose also noted that the entertainment's speed of execution and decibel level were as important as its content. "The band should be as loud as possible," he insisted. "The problem is to outshout the customers.... To do a nightclub show right is a speed trick.... Every act is cut to the bone. You have to keep in mind that 700 people are wrestling with a five course dinner. The goal is a down to earth show with obvious audience appeal... no subtlety allowed."[36] The Diamond Horseshoe adhered unswervingly to this formula all of its twelve years, relying almost entirely on old-time acts and a Gay Nineties ambience (fig. 23). The club featured many of the same acts in 1950 that had helped to establish it in 1938.

Rose's preoccupation with the Diamond Horseshoe led to a corresponding neglect of Casa Mañana, which soon experienced a significant drop in attendance. The club's *Streamlined Varieties* had, in fact, become embarrassingly sloppy. Problems began to crop up with performers missing cues and failing to appear for their acts. Several ushers had to be posted at the bar to ensure that Lou Holtz remained sober enough for the second show. As rumors of the club's decline spread in the local gossip columns, Rose announced that an entirely new show would be produced to take the place of the ill-fated variety bill.

On April 10, 1939, *The Big Show* opened at Casa Mañana. It was a typical Rose and Anderson revue that told "The Story of American Show Business" in four sequences: circus, vaudeville, cinema and television.[37] The show starred James Barton, whose presence had helped salvage Rose's *Sweet and Low* eight years before. Despite his stoutest efforts, Barton was unable to do the same for *The Big Show*.

As had been the case with Rose's touring fiasco *Show of Shows*, his staff was incredibly overworked. Between preparing for the New York World's Fair and opening the Diamond Horseshoe, Anderson, Alton, duBois and Johnson were unable to devote their full energies to the Casa Mañana revue. As the *New York News* put it, "The good acts are too familiar for novelty and the novelty acts just aren't good enough.... Far too many of the turns were at Casa Mañana last week or the week before that."[38] An exception to the evening's generally lackluster fare was provided by Jack Cole and his troupe, which performed a series of Balinese dances to both native and swing rhythms.

Tired material was hardly the club's only problem. Soon after *The Big Show* opened, Rose had to deal with a waiters' strike and a suit by Fred Fischer charging gross violations of the lease agreement. With his energies already divided between the fair and the Diamond Horseshoe, Rose was severely overextended. Five weeks after *The Big Show* opened, Rose closed Casa Mañana. Despite statements to the press that the club would be back in business after the fair, Casa Mañana never reopened.

Meanwhile, however, Rose's *Aquacade* had become a tremendous success at the fair (see chapter 6), and the Diamond Horseshoe was enjoying an even greater measure of popularity. *The Turn of the Century* was followed by a series of equally well received productions. The prewar shows included Texas Guinan in *Mrs. Astor's Pet Horse* (an offbeat tale of a carriage horse who once raced in the Kentucky Derby) and the only Diamond Horseshoe production conceived entirely by John Murray Anderson, *The Silver Screen*.[39]

Figure 23. Scenes from Diamond Horseshoe Revues, ca. 1948
(Courtesy Billy Rose Theatre Collection, New York Public Library, Astor, Lenox and Tilden Foundations)

The last Diamond Horseshoe show prior to America's entry into World War II, *The Silver Screen* opened in March of 1941. It was a lavish and sentimental pastiche of motion picture history. Noble Sissle and his orchestra played while representations of film personalities from the Keystone Kops to Greta Garbo (played by Mary Dowell in a long black dress) passed across the stage. The finale featured such old Hollywood stalwarts as Gilda Gray and Mae Murray accompanied by a chorus in Walt Disney cartoon character masks.

Some of the Diamond Horseshoe's most spirited offerings came during the war. Typical of these was *It's Fun to Be Free,* in which master of ceremonies George Jessel described the world conflict as "a war between people who insist on laughing and a people who can't laugh to save their souls."[40] The show included such diverse talents as Jack Benny, Eddie Cantor and Carmen Miranda. Bill "Bojangles" Robinson did a tap routine at a mock funeral for Adolf Hitler, and Ethel Merman sang "Any Bonds Today?" Another highlight featured Leo Durocher and several Brooklyn Dodgers joining Ella Logan for a few choruses of "Take Me Out to the Ballgame." One of the more interesting acts was the so-called "Refugee Revue," which was composed of German, Austrian and Polish variety performers who had escaped from the Nazis.[41]

After the war, Rose sensed that the Diamond Horseshoe's Gay Nineties format was beginning to grow stale. On a trip to Paris in 1947, he stopped at a restaurant called the Monseigneur in which several dozen violinists moved about the room serenading diners. Rose liked the idea and used it as the basis for a new show that he and Anderson wrote called *Violins over Broadway*. The Diamond Horseshoe's usual jazz ensemble was replaced by thirty-seven violins, four cellos, four violas, two harps, two pianos, a choral group and a brass section. A ballet corps performing on point replaced the usual showgirls.[42]

The show's program of classical favorites also precipitated a redecoration of the interior by Herman Rosse, who managed to impart some Viennese touches without completely abandoning Albert Johnson's decor. Anderson persuaded Rose to invest in elaborate new silverware and three-branch candelabra for the tables and red evening tailcoats for the violinists. The candelabra held tiny lightbulbs that provided the only illumination during the more romantic selections.

Although *Violins over Broadway* ran for two years, its success was not sufficient to reverse the Diamond Horseshoe's declining popularity. After covering its losses for several months, Rose closed the club early in 1951. Still, the Diamond Horseshoe was tremendously successful and had become a tourist attraction on the level of the Empire State Building and Times Square. During its twelve years of operation, more than four million people had seen its shows. John Murray Anderson later estimated that the Diamond Horseshoe grossed "in the neighborhood of twenty million dollars."[43]

The closing of the Diamond Horseshoe effectively ended the era of lavish nightclub productions in New York. Postwar America was changing significantly in ways that were felt but not yet understood in 1951. It was television that brought this new and disquieting world into people's homes, yet it was to television that Americans turned for escape. Ironically, many of the old Diamond Horseshoe performers, including Milton Berle and Jack Benny, became major entertainers in the early days of television. Once again the very success of a live theatrical form had led to its demise. Television co-opted nightclub acts in much the same way that movies had co-opted the theatre. Rose's style of entertainment had not lost its appeal; it had simply been adopted by a new medium. Just as Billy Rose had found a way to repackage traditional vaudeville, so television had found a way to repackage him.

Rose was unattuned to the new public sensibilities. Like many showmen, he was a creature of habit and superstition who found it hard to abandon anything that had ever been popular. If it had worked once, his reasoning went, it would work again. A country that could produce the 1939 New York World's Fair had not yet lost its penchant for fantasy on a grand scale. Although the conventions on which he had relied were losing their vitality, Rose still believed that he could do anything. His attitude was similar to that expressed by George M. Cohan who, when asked if he could "write a play without a flag," responded, "I could write a play without anything but a pencil."[44] Rose was one of the last of that particular breed of impresarios who, like Cohan, genuinely believed that nothing was impossible.

7

World's Fairs, 1939–1940

You will like the Fair.
You will thoroughly enjoy it.
You will like the plan of it—the layout—the design.
It is good theatre.
You will like the sweep of it—the marvelous effects—
  the lovely vistas—the gaiety—the color.
You will be astonished, amused, and enlightened—
To be on the stage, behind the scenes, and in the audience!
  1939 New York World's Fair souvenir program

The 1939 New York World's Fair was one of the most flamboyantly theatrical expositions in history. As Morton Eustis noted in his review of the fair for *Theatre Arts Monthly,* "To describe in detail all the exhibits which make use of theatre technique at the Fair—or which are, in themselves, dramatic— would require a volume."[1] The Fair's many live entertainments and elaborate dioramic environments (such as the General Motors Pavilion) provided an ideal backdrop for Billy Rose's style of spectacular amusement. Its scale was also something he could appreciate: two hundred pavilions and a projected first-year attendance of forty million people.

The fair was indeed a gargantuan undertaking. The 1200-acre site was fashioned from a smelly marsh in Queens described by F. Scott Fitzgerald in *The Great Gatsby* as "a valley of ashes—a fantastic farm where ashes grow like wheat into...grotesque gardens and...spasms of bleak dust."[2] Known appropriately as Flushing Meadows, the area contained a series of refuse heaps and swampy railroad easements bounded on the east by the equally foul Flushing River.

The clearance and improvement of this monumental garbage dump constituted the largest land reclamation project yet undertaken in the eastern United States. The selection of such an inhospitable site was due largely to the vigorous efforts of New York Parks Commissioner Robert Moses, who saw the fair as a means to develop an expansive new city park. For the first time in the history of international expositions, advance arrangements had been made to turn the site over to a local government at the end of the fair.[3]

From May of 1935, when the idea for the fair was first put forward by the Jackson Heights engineer Joseph Shagden, until its opening in April of 1939, the project required a total investment of nearly $160 million. New York was determined to surpass the expositions staged by other American cities. Chicago had presented two tremendously successful fairs in 1893 and 1933. Philadelphia, Saint Louis and San Francisco also had notable expositions to their credit. New York had not hosted a major fair since 1853, when it erected a halfhearted copy of London's Crystal Palace on the site of what is now Bryant Park and the New York Public Library.

The city was committed to the project through the enthusiasm of its flamboyant mayor, Fiorello La Guardia and the tireless efforts of fair president Grover Whalen. New York City also paid $27 million for site reclamation and permanent improvements and solicited a commitment of $35 million from foreign governments for the construction of the international pavilions. By the time Rose signed his agreement with Whalen on June 16, 1938, sixty nations and international organizations had agreed to participate in the fair, making it the most widely represented major exposition of the century.

Although *Let's Play Fair* had given Rose his opportunity at the New York World's Fair, the question of what he would do with the opportunity remained a mystery. His contract specified only that a synopsis of "the Project" was to be submitted by December 1, 1938. At the time, Whalen favored an entertainment that would lend credence to the fair's claim of celebrating the 150th anniversary of George Washington's inaugural.[4] To this end, Whalen and Rose discussed a musical extravaganza based on American history, which the contract tentatively titled "My Country 'Tis of Thee." Rose was willing to go along with the idea and rejected suggestions by John Murray Anderson and Eleanor Holm that he produce another *Aquacade*. He felt that after the Great Lakes Exposition in Cleveland (see chapter 4), people would consider another water show "old hat." Although Rose led Whalen and other officials to believe that an American theme pageant was feasible, there were countless problems with the idea. Privately, he had his doubts as to the viability of anything with too much history in it.

Rose did, however, make an effort to accommodate the historical yearnings of the fair's planners. He and Anderson devised a rough outline for a show entitled *The Voice of America*.[5] Anderson and duBois then spent a week in Atlantic City working out the design details and script for the project. They conceived a massive pageant that featured three revolving stages, escalators, moving platforms, steam curtains and a finale in which Mount Rushmore rose on elevators to form the concluding tableau. Although the estimates for the mechanical equipment alone were in the neighborhood of $250,000, Rose decided to present an outline of the show to Whalen and Moses, who was overseeing the soon-to-be-completed New York State Amphitheatre.

Moses was an imposing and contentious figure whose zest for conflict and publicity equaled Rose's. He had an unswerving belief in the need for civic dignity and a rigid sense of propriety. Moses lacked even a modicum of Grover Whalen's refinement and style; he was a veritable Caesar of public works whose vision of the fair did not include Billy Rose. To Moses, Rose was a greedy mountebank whose style of entertainment would cheapen the fair. Still, Moses agreed (at Whalen's urging) to hear Rose's proposal, which he later described as "a séance."[6]

Rose began his presentation with a series of large cartoon panels which illustrated his concept for a sweeping panorama of American history, a sort of living textbook à la Cecil B. De Mille. Moses became uneasy when Rose circulated the cartoons to the accompaniment of an animated nonstop narration. "The hand of God is over America," Rose exclaimed as he acted out the scene of Columbus setting foot on the shores of the new world. The pictures were flying fast and furious; Suwannee River, Washington crossing the Delaware, the covered wagons carrying the settlers west. Rose even imitated the sound of wagon wheels sloshing and banging over the trail. Moses thought things had definitely gotten out of hand.[7]

Rose had just begun reciting Lincoln's Gettysburg address when he stopped and exclaimed directly to Moses, "The voice of America breaks through!" He then removed a small harmonica from his pocket and began an impromptu rendition of several well-known American folk songs. Rose mixed his narration with a few frantic bars of various melodies until Moses was left in a state somewhere between shock and disbelief. Finally, after a rousing chorus of "America the Beautiful" on the mouth harp, Rose collapsed back into his chair. Whalen turned to Moses for his opinion, but the commissioner offered only a few, well-chosen expletives and left the room. It was Robert Moses's first encounter with Billy Rose and, to his everlasting distress, it would not be his last.[8]

Despite Moses's reservations, Whalen was satisfied with the project. John Murray Anderson, however, had his doubts. He knew that Rose intended to finance the project himself and felt that *The Voice of America* was simply too expensive to be a success. As the amphitheatre neared completion, Rose and Anderson drove out to see it. Anderson was immediately convinced that another *Aquacade* was the only feasible attraction to present in the huge facility. Constructing the pool and diving towers would be far less expensive than the elaborate equipment needed for the historical pageant. Rose remained unconvinced. He was certain that Moses and Whalen would find an *Aquacade* too undignified.

Anderson wisely decided to enlist the support of Eleanor Holm, who was already excited about the possibility of starring in a New York *Aquacade*. Lincoln Dickey, the manager of the Cleveland fair, added his counsel in favor of an *Aquacade*. Rose was beginning to realize that *The Voice of America* was unworkable, but still felt that something completely novel was in order. He knew that a decision was needed soon, as the production synopsis deadline was fast approaching.

In the fall of 1938, Rose told Whalen of his growing doubts about the historical show and offered a new idea called "Killers of the Deep," which he described as "*Jumbo* underwater with octopuses and sharks." He also proposed yet another variation on the Pioneer Palace theme, this time called The Barbary Coast. Rose soon abandoned the "Killers" idea when he learned the cost of obtaining the attraction's various exotic fish.

Rose was still undecided about the fair show in November and secured an extension for the submission of his proposal until January 24, 1939 (less than three months before the fair's scheduled opening). The question was soon resolved, however, when Eleanor Holm applied her persuasive talents to the situation. Rose also began to realize, as he later told Ward Morehouse, that "People don't want to see Revolutionary War hats. They want those tiny wet bathing suits." On November 17, Rose announced that he would produce an *Aquacade* at the New York World's Fair.[9]

Despite fears that Whalen would veto the idea, Rose had little trouble winning the fair president's confidence. For all his own noble visions of the fair, Whalen trusted Rose's instincts as a producer. Rose represented a side of show business that fascinated Whalen, and although he did not want to get too close to it, he saw its appeal from a popular point of view. He had also seen the balance sheets from Fort Worth and Cleveland and knew Rose to be an extremely effective promoter.

So Grover Whalen listened politely and with great interest while Billy Rose explained what the public wanted at a world's fair. To Rose, it was simple: fair goers wanted to eat, drink and look at nude or nearly nude girls. In between these cornerstones of fair life, they wanted color, music, noise and entertainment. The exposition should have the feel of circus and yet be more refined and polished—a show that the average person could enjoy and admire. Rose was concerned that the fair's proposed seventy-five cent general admission would severely limit attendance. "You fellows are talking about an attendance of 75 million," Rose pointedly told Whalen. "Where are your 75 million coming from? The Stork Club? Park Avenue?"[10] The way Rose saw it, people wanted a good time for a reasonable amount of money. This meant the fair would make money. Rose smiled at Whalen, "You want to make money, don't you Grover?"[11]

While Rose's decision to present the *Aquacade* simplified his dealings with the fair, it was a brief honeymoon. Robert Moses was opposed to the idea and told Rose in a letter that a temporary pool was out of the question for the amphitheatre and that a permanent one would cost $120,000. Although Rose was in fact able to construct the pool for half that, the amphitheatre itself was beset by a host of troubles. The 11,000-seat facility was plagued with cost overruns, labor problems and poor construction decisions. Several hundred pilings had to be replaced when it was discovered that portions of the foundation had been laid on improperly drained and leveled ground. Charges of featherbedding and contract fraud were so widespread that Governor Herbert H. Lehman was forced to appoint a commission to study the amphitheatre's management.

Logistical problems aside, Rose and Anderson pressed ahead with plans for the show. Since he also intended to produce his Barbary Coast saloon attraction, Rose wisely hired Lincoln Dickey to oversee the shows' daily operations and finances. He then announced an audition for swimmers at Madison Square Garden, which drew a crowd of 25,000 and required two hundred riot police to control. It was without doubt one of the largest and most chaotic chorus calls in Broadway history.

Fifteen hundred of the more attractive applicants were eventually selected for serious consideration. After several days, the list was reduced to three hundred performers who were then auditioned at the swimming pool of the Saint George Hotel. Thinking their problems reduced to a manageable level, Rose and Anderson were shocked to find that nearly one hundred of the finalists had lied and could not swim a stroke. Several had to be rescued from the pool.[12] A union delegate asked Rose about the dismissal of a particular chorine. "Isn't she good enough for you?" he inquired. "No," Rose responded brusquely, "she sinks."[13] The remainder of the swimming chorus was drawn from local high school and college swim teams.

Securing the rest of the show's talent was slightly less problematic. Johnny Weissmuller agreed to return as Holm's costar, as did many of the best divers from the Cleveland *Aquacade*. As with previous Rose productions, numerous crackpot acts also offered their services. One man billed himself as The Human Aircraft Carrier, and claimed to be unsinkable. To prove the point, he leaped into the pool with a hundred-pound weight on his back and immediately plunged to the bottom. After several swimmers barely managed to pull him to the surface, the man looked up at Rose and shrugged, "No harm in trying."[14]

Although Albert Johnson, Raoul Pène duBois and the rest of the production staff completed their designs and preparations with the usual efficiency, the New York State Amphitheatre continued to encounter difficulties. The huge pool required an elaborate heating and filtration system that was constructed by a union firm in Connecticut. Because of an obscure contract provision, the amphitheatre's union contractors insisted on dismantling the completed system and having their crews reassemble and install it. Rose rightly claimed that this would delay the pool's completion several weeks and would force his cast to work under unsanitary and potentially dangerous conditions. The union was adamant, even though Rose offered to pay the $10,000 in wages that the task would involve. As a result, the cast worked for weeks in freezing putrid water that gave many of the swimmers severe earaches and rashes.[15]

The additional construction costs and delays were just the beginning of Rose's union troubles. As was his usual practice, Rose signed many of the young swimmers to contracts that did not include rehearsal pay. When the cast tried to organize and force Rose's hand, he claimed that the additional expense would bankrupt the show before it opened. Threats and counterthreats ensued until the dispute was arbitrated, and Rose agreed to the performers' demands for rehearsal pay.

At times, the show's problems seemed certain to bring it down. Rose had to spend an entire day talking a plumbing contractor out of a $45,000 overtime charge. Less than a week before the show opened, all of the costumes burned and had to be redone by crews working triple shifts. Rose and Anderson, normally amiable as collaborators go, were at each other's throats on several occasions. During one argument Rose bellowed, "I've got a fistful of money. What have you got?" As the cast held its breath, Anderson coldly replied, "I have one friend."[16] Despite such outbursts, the two managed to survive rehearsals with their working relationship intact.

From the beginning of his association with the fair until its close in 1940, Rose was continually at odds with Robert Moses. Even Whalen, who had settled 130 labor disputes as National Recovery Administration director, failed to prevent the clash of these two formidable egos. The most outstanding of their disputes centered on Rose's approach to advertising. Approximately two months before the show's opening, Rose secured Whalen's permission to erect a large electric sign at the Amphitheatre that read "BILLY ROSE'S *AQUACADE*" in eight-foot letters. Rose paid $12,000 for the sign and was preparing to install it when Moses intervened. He refused to allow the sign to go up and told Rose that "the New York State Amphitheatre will not be a stepping stone to your glory."[17]

In a typical countermove, Rose went to the amphitheatre at four o'clock the following morning with a crew of electricians and put up the sign. He also posted men with baseball bats to prevent its removal. Moses responded by threatening to call in the New York state militia. After several days of virulent press statements by both men, Governor Lehman offered to mediate the dispute. As usual, Rose was fully prepared for the session. To counter the charge that he was only interested in self-promotion, Rose had photographs taken of all the parks and civic projects that prominently featured Moses's name on plaques and billboards. He also prepared slides of the GM, Ford and GE pavilions, all of which showed the corporations' names in huge letters.

Rose maintained that his sign was simply in keeping with other concessionaires' promotional activities. He concluded his argument to Lehman with a gag that won the day. "I think I could satisfy the Parks Commissioner in five minutes by changing a single letter in that sign," Rose quipped. "Instead of Rose's *Aquacade* it would be Moses *Aquacade*."[18]

Despite seemingly endless setbacks, the *Aquacade* opened on May 5, only five days after the fair's official debut. Fortunately for Rose and his staff, it was essentially the same show they had staged in Cleveland two years earlier. There were several new songs and some additional specialty numbers, but the script remained basically unchanged. However, since the production now had the benefit of a much larger theatre, the aquatic and chorus sequences were a good deal more elaborate. Paul Whiteman and his orchestra occupied space under one diving tower while Fred Waring's Glee Club chorus sang from the other.[19] The stage and costume effects were also more spectacular. The water curtain at the original *Aquacade* was replaced by an 8000-gallon-per-minute system that created a veil of mist 260 feet wide and 40 feet high. As in Cleveland, the water curtain was turned on before the show while the audience took its seats. Then, in the words of the program, "the signal is given, an unseen hand pulls a switch, the wall of water drops, and the show in all its magnificent beauty is revealed."[20]

What was revealed were two hundred swimmers, once again referred to as Aquabelles and Aquabeaux (nonswimming cast members were called Aquagals and Aquadudes). In the opening sequence, they lined up across the edge of the stage in shimmering skintight suits, stood for ten seconds, and then began a precision dominolike plunge into the pool (fig. 24). The show then quickly moved through a series of elaborate swimming and diving routines accompanied by the music of Paul Whiteman's orchestra and a good deal of land-bound pageantry.

The first of the show's four scenes was set at "A Beach in Florida" and featured Frances Williams singing "It Happened in Miami," while a chorus of Aquagals performed on stage with beach balls, and swimmers cavorted in the pool (fig. 25).[21] In the second scene Morton Downey introduced Eleanor Holm to the strains of "Yours for a Song," while she and Weissmuller performed a precision swimming duet in the center of the pool. The scene also featured a mass roller-skating routine similar to the one originally done in Cleveland. As eighty Aquadudes and Aquagals skated back and forth (fig. 26), Holm sang a Rose-Suesse composition entitled "Roller Skating on a Rainbow." The scene concluded with a diving exhibition in which eight Olympic divers performed simultaneously on the theatre's two diving platforms.[22]

Each of the swimming numbers concluded with the cast paddling off-stage through an opening underneath the bandstand, which also doubled as a diving platform. While the swimmers changed costumes, Aquaclown Stubby

Figure 24. Opening Scene from the *Aquacade,* 1939 New York World's Fair
*(Courtesy Billy Rose Theatre Collection, New York Public Library,
Astor, Lenox and Tilden Foundations)*

Krueger performed, along with the knockabout farce team of Willie, West and McGinty. Their ill-fated attempt to construct a house was extremely well received, as Brooks Atkinson noted: "Given some boards, ladders, saws, hammers and saw-horses and a general air of concentrated shiftlessness, they can roar you as hilariously as a convention of clowns."[23]

Another highlight was the appearance of Gertrude Ederle, who in 1926 had become the first woman to swim the English Channel. Ederle, who was nearly deaf, could not hear the applause and thought for weeks that her swim went unappreciated. During one performance, however, her ears cleared briefly and she heard for the first and only time the thunderous reaction of the crowd. The experience was overwhelming. "I heard it!" she sobbed to Eleanor Holm backstage. "Tonight I heard it!"[24]

In the third scene John Murray Anderson and Robert Alton once again presented their self-partnering chorus routine (see chapter 4), employing twice

Figure 25. Beach Ball Scene from the *Aquacade*, 1939 New York World's Fair *(Courtesy Billy Rose Theatre Collection, New York Public Library, Astor, Lenox and Tilden Foundations)*

Figure 26. Roller Skating Scene from the *Aquacade*, 1939 New York World's Fair *(Courtesy Billy Rose Theatre Collection, New York Public Library, Astor, Lenox and Tilden Foundations)*

as many girls as had appeared in Cleveland. The final section was devoted almost entirely to aquatic sequences, including additional appearances by Holm and Weissmuller. The finale featured a parade of state banners that culminated when a huge American flag was spread across the steep, Ziegfeld-style staircase at the rear of the stage. Rose had long subscribed to George M. Cohan's theory that failure was impossible while waving the flag.

The New York reviewers immediately proclaimed the *Aquacade* Rose's greatest triumph, and indeed it seemed to have an almost hypnotic effect on those who saw it. Phrases such as "vision of loveliness," "unsurpassed beauty" and "supreme achievement" were common. The larger scale of the New York version and the increased complexity of the swimming formations made the show's visual impact all the more arresting. "I enjoyed the same satisfying thrill watching... [the *Aquacade*] that I had from seeing... Sonja Henie's ice ballet," commented Burns Mantle. "[The swimmers'] bobbing heads and flashing arms cleave the water in unison, as the bows of a string orchestra rise and descend to the baton of their leader. A fine effect."[25] "The *Aquacade* ought to be good summer entertainment in any man's town," wrote Brooks Atkinson, "with or without a World's Fair to serve as bazaar and backdrop."[26]

On top of its lavish production, Rose's spectacle was also a good value. Tickets ranged from general admission at forty cents to a top price of only $1.00. Despite the low admission charge, the *Aquacade* frequently grossed more than $150,000 a week.[27] Lines nearly twenty blocks long were not uncommon, even in bad weather. Rose later noted that, "the biggest star of the *Aquacade* was a thing called 40 cents."[28]

While price was unquestionably a factor, Rose's promotional efforts for the *Aquacade* also contributed to its success. He was determined to prove his oft-repeated contention that "Promotion is the biggest part of the show business next to girls."[29] From having Johnny Weissmuller select a "Tarzan Junior" three times a day (fig. 27), to staging the nuptials of two of his performers in a hotel swimming pool, Rose seldom missed an opportunity to ballyhoo his show (fig. 28). When reporters asked if the cast had time to eat, what with four shows a day, he responded with a shot of several Aquabelles dining at a floating table (fig. 29). Rose made frequent product endorsements, including lending his name and likeness to a Spam advertisement in the *Aquacade* program (fig. 30). According to Lucius Beebe, this particular endorsement proved conclusively that "Billy Rose is indeed in the business of selling meat of questionable character."[30] Although Rose received a certain amount of criticism for excessive merchandising, few people doubted that the *Aquacade* itself was an elegant and eminently tasteful show. It was ironic that Rose, the great purveyor of risqué girlie shows, had managed to promote the *Aquacade* as a chaste and wholesome production.

For once, Rose was in the position of offering a refined alternative to the kind of attractions his nightclubs had featured for years. He no doubt relished

Figure 27. Johnny Weissmuller, 1939
(Courtesy Billy Rose Theatre Collection, New York Public Library, Astor, Lenox and Tilden Foundations)

the fact that, while the *Aquacade* earned nearly unanimous praise, John Krimsky's side shows were giving the rest of the fair's amusement zone a bad name. Typical of these blatantly prurient amusements was "Arctic Girl's Tomb of Ice," a carnivalesque feature perhaps best described in the fair's official program:

> Clad in an an abbreviated bathing suit, a beautiful girl is entombed in a solid cake of crystal-clear ice.... Special lighting and the clearness of the ice enable you to observe the Arctic Girl closely, and by means of a microphone and amplifiers you may converse with her. Only her ability to produce self-hypnosis makes possible this seeming, icy contradiction.[31]

Such seedy entertainments angered many who felt that the fair's lofty goals were being compromised. *New York Post* columnist Westbrook Pegler lamented the presence at the fair of

> Lewd, lascivious, indecent and vicious exhibitions by naked or near-naked women, some of whom would be called dancers, while others would not pretend to dance but would just frolic about in public with nothing on.... This type of theater has been a pain and a shame

Figure 28. *Aquacade* Publicity Stunt, 1939 New York World's Fair
(Courtesy Billy Rose Theatre Collection, New York Public Library, Astor, Lenox and Tilden Foundations)

to the decent element of show business for many years, a twilight zone in which trollops and procurers operate in the guise of actors.... Maybe it's the un-American influence of the foreigners who just won't get assimilated.[32]

Pegler's outrage was shriller than most, but it was indicative of the problems encountered by the rest of the amusement zone. Other articles and reports on the zone portrayed it as a second-class collection of side shows that hurt the rest of the fair. In reality, however, the fair's problems had more to do with its high admission price than with the character of its entertainment. People attended the *Aquacade* not only because it was a spectacular and superbly realized production, but because it cost only forty cents to get in.

As a result, Rose's show was making more money than the rest of the fair's entertainments combined. In fact, many other attractions were operating at a considerable loss. Mike Todd's various ventures at the fair (including *The Hot Mikado* with Bill Robinson and a jazzed-up version of the Shuberts' Broadway revue, *Streets of Paris*) lost close to one million dollars.

Figure 29. *Aquacade* Publicity Stunt, 1939 New York World's Fair
(Courtesy Billy Rose Theatre Collection, New York Public Library, Astor, Lenox and Tilden Foundations)

Figure 30. *Aquacade* Advertisement, 1939 New York World's Fair Souvenir Program
(Courtesy Billy Rose Theatre Collection, New York Public Library, Astor, Lenox and Tilden Foundations)

Figure 31. Salvador Dali's *Dream of Venus*, New York World's Fair, 1940 *(Courtesy Billy Rose Theatre Collection, New York Public Library, Astor, Lenox and Tilden Foundations)*

George Jessel was similarly unsuccessful with an attraction called "Little Old New York" that attempted to play on the popularity of Rose's Diamond Horseshoe. Perhaps the most intriguing failure was Salvador Dali's *Dream of Venus,* a lurid assemblage of surrealist sculpture in a walk-through environment that featured a couch in the shape of Greta Garbo's lips (fig. 31).

The amusement zone's lackluster showing was hardly Whalen's only problem. Despite the great success of the *Aquacade* and the excellent notices garnered by the fair as a whole, Grover Whalen's great festival of the future closed its first season solidly in the red. Attendance figures were not up to expectations, and many people were offended by the less-than-refined nature of Krimsky's midway. Sally Rand's appearance at the fair added to the popular notion that Whalen was letting things get out of hand. Although he remained fair president for the 1940 season, effective control of programming fell to Harvey Gibson (president of Manufacturers Hanover Trust), who had been the fair's finance chairman.

Gibson was determined to tone down the more ribald aspects of the amusement zone while at the same time stressing those portions of the fair that appealed to the broadest possible audience. Whalen's lofty notions of the future and international brotherhood were being swept aside by the widening war in Europe and Gibson's determination to attract a crowd by whatever means the budget and popular taste would permit.

In an effort to revitalize the amusement zone, Gibson wanted to dismiss Krimsky and offer Rose the job of amusement director. Despite Gibson's strenuous lobbying, Rose refused to consider the proposition. He felt that Gibson had unfairly usurped Whalen's authority and would have nothing to do with him. Despite his image as a ruthless opportunist, Rose was loyal to Whalen, who had stuck by him in his disputes with Moses and other fair officials. "In show business there are what we call right guys and wrong guys," Rose told Gibson. "Grover is a right guy, and I really don't have to say what that makes you."[33]

Rose further demonstrated his dislike for Gibson by withdrawing all of the *Aquacade*'s proceeds (roughly two million dollars) from Gibson's bank. Despite Rose's opposition, Gibson was determined to make the 1940 season a success, although his new slogan for the fair, "Peace and Freedom," seemed both naïve and highly inappropriate given the deteriorating world situation. Still, the fair trudged gamely ahead. With forty million dollars in outstanding bonds, it could hardly do otherwise.

Rose and Anderson made few changes in the *Aquacade* for its second season. The 1940 version replaced Johnny Weissmuller with Buster Crabbe (star of the Flash Gordon movie serial) and added several new production numbers (including scenes depicting the 1925 Paris and 1933 Chicago world's fairs) that were adapted from the Fort Worth Casa Mañana.[34] The show might have included fresher material had not Rose's attention been diverted by developments elsewhere.

In 1938, he had been approached by representatives of the 1939 Golden Gate Exposition. The promoters of the San Francisco fair asked Rose if he would be interested in staging an *Aquacade* at the exposition. Rose, who was then solely concerned with producing a show for the New York World's Fair, declined the offer. Shortly after the New York fair closed its first season, Rose received a phone call from a reporter named Barney Gould who had interviewed him in San Francisco some years earlier. Gould told Rose that Jules Stein, president of the Music Corporation of America, had made detailed photographs of the New York *Aquacade* and was planning to stage a copy at the San Francisco fair in 1940. Stein's powerful operation controlled the booking for many of the nation's most popular bands and entertainers. As such, he had the tacit backing of Bay area hotel owners, whose cooperation was vital to the success of any fair.

Always intensely conscious of any attempt to steal his material, Rose dispatched Lincoln Dickey to San Francisco to investigate the potential threat. He authorized Dickey to do anything necessary to stop the Stein production, including proposing a San Francisco *Aquacade*. After examining plans and blueprints for the production, Dickey concluded that Stein's *Treasure Island Water Follies* was indeed a nearly exact copy of the *Aquacade*. He also learned that Stein had convinced the city to provide most of the backing for the show. Dickey then went to San Francisco Mayor Angelo J. Rossi and bluntly asked him, "Do you want Jules Stein to steal Rose's *Aquacade* and produce it with your money or would you rather have Billy Rose do the original with his?"[35]

While the mayor and other exposition officials pondered Dickey's offer, Rose wrote an advertisement for *Variety* that recalled his lambasting of the Shuberts fifteen years earlier. It began:

> STOP THIEF!
>
> A social climber, a mental pickpocket,
> a herring eater with a society complex is
> trying to steal Billy Rose's *Aquacade!*[36]

Rose never had the opportunity to see his invective in print, for shortly after Dickey's meeting with the mayor, the Golden Gate Exposition agreed to negotiate with Rose for a production of the *Aquacade*. In addition to a number of other lucrative provisions, Rose's contract stated that Jules Stein was not permitted to book any attractions at the fair. "He can't even have a strolling guitar player on the grounds," Rose gloated.[37]

The San Francisco fair, although hardly on a scale with its New York counterpart, was constructed on an even more unlikely site: an island in San Francisco Bay created specifically for the event. Named Treasure Island, it was built up from a formation known as the Yerba Buena Shoals, a ten-foot-deep shallows lying just to the west of Yerba Buena Island between San Francisco and Oakland. The U.S. Army Corps of Engineers spent eighteen months filling the shoals with Bay sand and concrete to create a 400-acre artificial island, which was to be turned over to the city after the fair for use as an airport.

The fair's theme focused on the history and cultures of the Pacific. Its overall design featured a highly eclectic combination of "Mayan, Incan, Malayan and Cambodian architecture."[38] While visually fascinating and generally well-executed, such architectural oddities were not enough to ensure the exposition's success. As was the case with many fairs of the 1930s the exposition's promoters found themselves in precarious financial straits at the end of their first season. Although attendance had been respectable, numerous claims by the fair's creditors threatened its solvency. The exposition was able to postpone many of its debt payments on the promise that more popular and profitable entertainments would be added for the 1940 season. It was hoped that the *Aquacade* would do for Treasure Island what it had done previously for New York and Cleveland.

Rose's third *Aquacade* had to make do with a more modest setting than it had enjoyed in New York and Cleveland. The cramped Treasure Island fair site and unpredictable San Francisco weather made an outdoor *Aquacade* impossible. Rose had to settle for a large rectangular building that had been the International Hall during the 1939 season. His contract called for him to make all necessary improvements, including the pool, at his own expense, in return for which the fair would not receive its percentage of the gate until Rose had recovered his initial investment.[39]

Although strategically situated in the middle of the fairgrounds, the building was hardly the ideal site for a theatrical spectacle. It was a long narrow structure, the interior of which resembled an immense Quonset hut. John Murray Anderson likened it to a boxcar with a curved roof. Even allowing for a much smaller pool and a shallower stage, Rose was only able to achieve a maximum seating capacity of 7000, roughly 4000 fewer than in New York.

The construction of the pool proved to be the show's biggest problem. Due to the various structural difficulties presented by the building and its inadequate foundation, a concrete or steel pool was out of the question. The solution was provided by assembling a huge (200 feet long by 60 feet wide) wooden barge and caulking its seams to keep the water in. While such a design was cost-effective, it proved difficult to keep clean. Several performers later contracted ear infections that led to permanent hearing impairment.

With several notable exceptions, the show was an almost exact replica of the 1939 New York *Aquacade*. The cast was obviously reduced, and much of the scenery had to be modified to travel and fit into the smaller hall (fig. 32). And although Johnny Weissmuller had agreed to join the San Francisco production, Rose had to find a replacement for Eleanor Holm who, after marrying Rose in November 1939, preferred to remain with the New York *Aquacade*.

Rose and Anderson seemed unable to solve this particular casting dilemma. With only two weeks to go before the fair's opening, they found an attractive eighteen-year-old who was modeling bathing suits in a Los Angeles department store. The girl turned out to hold several national swimming titles, which was enough to convince Rose and Anderson to engage her on the spot. The following day the *San Francisco Chronicle* made a brief mention of Rose's new cast member in a one-column update of fair events: "Billy Rose announced last night that shapely Esther Williams of Los Angeles, holder of three national swimming titles, had deserted her amateur standing to become 'Aquabelle #1.'"[40]

With Williams in place, the San Francisco *Aquacade* opened on May 25

Figure 32. *Aquacade*, 1940 Golden Gate International Exposition
(*Courtesy California Historical Society, San Francisco*)

Figure 33. Finale of *Aquacade*, 1940 Golden Gate International Exposition (*Courtesy California Historical Society, San Francisco*)

to even greater praise than the New York and Cleveland shows (fig. 33). "The crowd applauds until it becomes hoarse," noted the *San Francisco Chronicle*. "They were swept to ecstatic heights by the sheer novelty; the superb rhythm... the twinkling, split-second routines performed by beauteous girls and their handsome escorts."[41] Rose's show was equally popular at the box office. The *Aquacade* recovered its initial investment of $600,000 by July and was ultimately seen by forty-one percent of all fair goers.[42] By the time the Golden Gate Exposition closed, Rose's three *Aquacade*s had been seen by more than fifteen million people and had become the most popular world's fair entertainments of all time.[43]

But the very triumph of the *Aquacade*s signaled the end of an era in exposition entertainments. World's fairs would never again achieve the grandeur and impact of the great prewar expositions. After the New York and San Francisco fairs closed, there was not another major international exposition for eighteen years.[44]

Television and films had begun to threaten both traditional outdoor amusements and the lavish nightclub revues discussed in the previous chapter. Rose was well aware that the new amusement technologies would ultimately spell the end of many old-time live popular entertainments. "The movies peddle millions of dollars worth of girls, music and scenery for 50 cents a look," he noted. "You can no longer get two bits for a quick peek at a flabby bimbo in a grass skirt. How can all these stale Cuban and Indian villages compete with a technicolor movie?"[45] Although Rose had not completely written off world's fairs, he did see their limitations. "The ultimate fraud in connection with all fairs is to sell bonds as if it were a genuine investment," he insisted. "It is impossible to amortize such costs in the running time of the average fair."[46]

On top of his doubts about the future of expositions, Rose needed a rest. Since the production of *Jumbo* in 1935, he had spent five intense years moving nonstop from one spectacular project to another. Now that he and Holm were married, Rose wanted to enjoy the financial rewards of his recent successes. He purchased an opulent Beekman Place brownstone and began outfitting it with as many famous works of art as his pocketbook would permit. Rose continued to occupy himself with the Diamond Horseshoe and occasionally mused to the press about his "imminent retirement" from show business. Few people took such declarations seriously. As one reporter succinctly put it, "Billy Rose can retire from show business in about the same way a fish can retire from the ocean."[47]

8

The War and After

Rose's self-proclaimed retirement from show business was predictably short-lived. Soon after his honeymoon, he became restless and began looking for new worlds to conquer. Despite frequent admissions that straight plays were not his forte, Rose's brief absence from the theatre had rekindled the urge to produce "serious" drama. Although his career was now at its peak, Rose's long-standing insecurity about the legitimate stage had never really dissipated. He believed that his more refined acquaintances would never accept him until he produced plays of lasting merit. Rose knew that his talents lay in less sophisticated entertainments but felt compelled to prove himself a worthy producer of dignified and intellectually credible theatre.

One reason that Rose had always favored nightclubs and spectacles over conventional plays was his own extremely short attention span. He was forever impatient with things that could not be explained and understood quickly. Still, Rose was possessed of the need to surpass his previous enterprises, and realized that he could only accomplish this by engaging in something completely different. Attempting to outdo the *Aquacade* would be a fruitless endeavor. He also knew that, for all its popularity, the *Aquacade* had been drained of its last bit of novelty and potential profit.

Rose also required a project more suited to his newly elevated lifestyle. Although his basic love of popular entertainment had not diminished, he now had to cultivate an air of respectability appropriate to his Beekman Place address. Since he and Holm had moved to their opulent new residence, Rose had become absorbed in the more refined aspects of Western culture. Ever since he first took notes for Bernard Baruch in 1917, Rose had longed to be a part of the world that the elegant Baruch personified. Now he began to learn about art, antique furniture, fine china and the correct way to serve claret.

When the opportunity arose in 1940 to back the Theatre Guild's production of Ernest Hemingway's *The Fifth Column*, Rose jumped at the chance. Although he was then readying productions for the second seasons of the New York and San Francisco world's fairs, Rose decided to take a chance with the project. As with his earlier enthusiasm for *The Great Magoo*, the content of the play and the quality of its writing mattered little. It was the names that were important. With Lee Strasberg directing a distinguished Theatre Guild cast in Hemingway's first stage play, Rose felt he had a sure thing.

Hemingway wrote *The Fifth Column*, his only full-length play, in Madrid during the Spanish Civil War when he was a war correspondent and champion of the loyalist cause. "It was written in the fall and early winter of 1937 while we were expecting an offensive," he recalled. "While we waited, I wrote the play... while writing, the hotel where we lived and worked was struck by more than thirty high explosive shells. So if it is not a good play perhaps that is what is the matter with it."[1]

Jed Harris originally picked up the option for the play but never felt that the script was strong enough to produce. Sensing the play's potential problems, Hemingway gave the script to Benjamin Glazer, who had successfully adapted Ferenc Molnar's *Liliom* for Broadway. After a fairly extensive rewrite, Glazer took the play to Lee Strasberg, who thought that the Theatre Guild might be interested. An initial reading of Glazer's adaptation convinced Strasberg that the play had been substantially improved. "Hemingway's original was an hour too long," he noted. "Glazer's moved logically and seemed better than the original, so we went into rehearsal with that."[2]

Strasberg assembled a stellar cast that included Lee J. Cobb, Franchot Tone and Lenore Ulric. During the show's protracted out-of-town tryouts, they began to realize that although Glazer's adaptation was a smoother and more polished piece of work, it lacked the impact and power of the Hemingway original. "Lee and I began to discard pages of the Glazer script and replace it with Hemingway's original work," Franchot Tone recalled. "Unfortunately Glazer and the Theatre Guild objected strenuously and a perpetual tug-of-war developed." Despite the fact that it launched him as a major star, Lee J. Cobb agreed that the script had its problems. "*The Fifth Column* was not Hemingway at all," he later told A. E. Hotchner. "At least not what we wound up with."[3] Although Hemingway's experience with *The Fifth Column* soured him on playwriting, he later acknowledged that Glazer's improvements had harmed the work as much as his own lack of dramatic expertise. "If being written under fire makes for defects," he told Hotchner, "it may also give a certain vitality."

When *The Fifth Column* opened in New York on March 6, at the Alvin Theatre, the reviewers praised the acting while questioning the script's viability as a play. Despite the excellent work of Cobb, Ulric and Tone, the show closed after eighty-seven performances (fig. 34). Richard Watts concisely summed up the problems in his review: "Something of Hemingway has gone out of it and something of Hollywood has gone in."[4] Strasberg remained convinced that Hemingway's original could have been successful,

Figure 34. Scene from the New York Production of *The Fifth Column*, 1940 (*Courtesy Billy Rose Theatre Collection, New York Public Library, Astor, Lenox and Tilden Foundations*)

but Armina Marshall of the Theatre Guild later said flatly, "Hemingway was a novelist not a playwright."[5]

Glazer was convinced that Rose might have salvaged the play by taking a more active role in the production. But despite his interest in the show, Rose was too overworked to spare much time for *The Fifth Column*. When Glazer pleaded with him to intervene, Rose was frank. "There is no possible way for me to work on *The Fifth Column* personally," he wrote. "I have four musicals in rehearsal simultaneously, and two of them are *Aquacades*.... I can only check off *The Fifth Column* to experience and write off the loss.... I agree with you completely—but what the hell! Just another show and just another lesson."[6] Glazer also felt that the show might survive on the road, but Rose had no such illusions. "With the first breath of summer," he predicted, "*The Fifth Column* will curl up like a pretzel."[7]

Despite *The Fifth Column*'s less than stupendous reception, Rose still hoped to broaden his horizons as a producer. Although he wrote an article for *Stage* magazine soon after the show's demise, entitled "Why I'm Not a Legit

Producer," Rose obviously harbored ambitions to the contrary. He had recently struck up a friendship with Clifford Odets, who had moved into an apartment on Beekman Place next to Rose's. Earlier in his career, after the success of *Waiting for Lefty,* Odets had become involved in a number of moneymaking Hollywood projects. The one-time champion of the left, who had once written of "the stormbirds of the middle class," now asked Rose's advice as to which champagnes to lay in for the winter and where to buy the best beluga caviar. Odets's increasing wealth and notoriety were also distancing him from the Group Theatre, which at the time was in a state of virtual dissolution. Although he was well aware, as Harold Clurman put it, "that the Group, for all its faults, had helped create him as much as he had helped create it," he was eager for new opportunities.[8]

During the summer and fall of 1940, Odets began work on a new play and read scenes from it to Rose as they were completed. Mesmerized by Odets's writing, Rose failed to see that, for all its deft characterizations, the new work rested on a stale and thoroughly clichéd plot. Entitled *Clash by Night,* the play concerned a love triangle with vague allusions to *Othello.* When a burly but childlike husband finds his beautiful wife carrying on with a movie projectionist, he strangles the rival in the projection booth against a background of light movie music and audience laughter.

Although a number of Rose's friends, including Moss Hart and Ben Hecht, tried to convince him otherwise, Rose was determined to produce the play. Richard Maney told him frankly that it was "hack writing," but Rose was unmoved. He was certain that the play's faults could be mended with a little of his usual jazzing up. "I'll have two colored pianists playing boogie-woogie in the pit during intermission," he told Maney, who replied, "Sure, that'll do wonders for the second act."[9] Rose never resorted to this gimmick, but it was a clear indication of his belief that any show could be improved with a shot of nightclub-style frivolity.

After hiring Strasberg to direct, Rose and Odets turned their attentions to casting. Against strong advice from his two collaborators, Odets insisted that the leading role of the unfaithful wife be played by Tallulah Bankhead. Although her Alabama drawl seemed out of place in a play set in Staten Island, Odets finally convinced his associates to go along with the choice. While Strasberg and Odets assembled the rest of the cast, Rose went about the daunting task of convincing the haughty and temperamental Bankhead to take the part.

The roster of American theatrical notables would have to be searched assiduously to find two less compatible people than Billy Rose and Tallulah Bankhead. Their vast differences in style and deportment were intensified by great mutual disdain and a shared love for flamboyant insults. In the realm of repartee, Rose had more than met his match; he endured several weeks of scathing invective before he finally convinced Bankhead to play the role. "You're a song and dance man, Rose, what the hell do you know about the theatre," she told him on one occasion. "I'm not one of your $25 a week Diamond Horseshoe floozies.... I was starring in plays on the London stage before you were eating herring at Lindy's."[10]

Bankhead's moody and mercurial personality made a problematic play all the more difficult to rehearse. Even her co-stars Lee J. Cobb and Joseph Schildkraut were not immune from her wrath. Cobb threatened to quit after Bankhead repeatedly interrupted one of his monologues with snapping fingers and irritated whispers of "Hurry up, you big ham!"[11] Nothing satisfied her. The costumes were "abominable" and the sets (by Boris Aronson) "miserable." Just before the show's out-of-town opening in Detroit, Rose noticed an error on the theatre's marquee:

> Billy Rose Present
> Tallulah Bankhead
> in
> *Clash by Night*

The omission of the "s" after "Present" prompted Bankhead's comment to Rose, "Either you put up a new bill with my name on top, or that sign might as well read: Billy Rose Present, Tallulah Bankhead Absent."[12] Rose's reluctant surrender of top billing hardly ended his troubles. Bankhead caught a cold in Detroit that delayed the Philadelphia opening by a week, during which time she refused to attend even brief rehearsals. Odets also had problems with Bankhead, who insisted on changing lines she disliked and padding her longer speeches. Each time Strasberg and Odets confronted her with this complaint, Bankhead would throw back her head and exclaim, "I'm in a nest of murderers."[13]

The real murderers turned out to be the press. "I'm at a loss to account for the motives of any of the talented people responsible for the appearance of *Clash by Night*," wrote Wolcott Gibbs in *The New Yorker*. "Did Billy Rose really imagine that he was performing an artistic service in producing this conspicuously dull and pretentious play?"[14] Brooks Atkinson was somewhat more polite, and wrote that, while Odets had "a genius for character and dialogue, his theme is commonplace."[15] Burns Mantle said simply that the play contained "uninteresting and unsympathetic subjects and is completely unrelieved in mood and tone."[16]

Rose took the play's savaging in stride. Soon after the reviews appeared, he sent the major New York critics each a bottle of champagne and a smoked turkey. "Having asked you to sit before one turkey," he wrote in the accompanying note, "permit me to send you another."[17] Although the press was quick to praise the work of the three stars, the show never caught on and closed on February 7 after only forty-three performances. While an active publicity push might have kept the play going, at that point Rose had little interest in saving *Clash by Night*. Although many Broadway sages attributed its demise to Tallulah Bankhead's temper, Rose had simply turned his attentions to a new and (for him) totally different project.

In the spring of 1942, as tales of Nazi atrocities against the Jews began to reach America, Ben Hecht decided to bring the tragic situation to the attention of the nation. He consulted with Rose and Moss Hart, and the three men met in George Kaufman's living room with thirty of the most prominent Jewish figures in show business. Hecht told the group of his plan to write and present a pageant in Madison Square Garden that would dramatize the ongoing Nazi genocide and raise money for the efforts to secure a Jewish homeland in Palestine. The response was enthusiastic. Kurt Weill offered to write the music for the show, which Rose would produce and Hart direct. Rose, Hecht, Weill and Hart also agreed to underwrite any losses from the production. By the end of the year, Hecht had completed the script and the show was ready to begin rehearsals.

Entitled *We Will Never Die,* the pageant opened at Madison Square Garden on March 9, 1943. Rose, employing his typical approach to publicity, convinced New York Governor Thomas Dewey to declare an official day of mourning for holocaust victims to coincide with the opening. A second show had to be added when the 20,000 tickets were sold within hours after they went on sale. Thousands of people who could not get tickets waited outside and listened to the show through loudspeakers. Hecht later wrote that the audience

> wanted to hear something that was not being spoken very loudly in our country.... Neither our government nor our busy commentators have concerned themselves to any extent with the fact that the Germans have already killed 2 million Jews and that they are engaged today and tomorrow in killing the 4 million Jews still surviving in German held territory.[18]

As presented at Madison Square Garden (and later in Washington, Chicago and other cities), the pageant took place against a backdrop of two huge tablets inscribed in Hebrew with the Ten Commandments. The actors, chorus and orchestra were arrayed on a huge stage in front of the tablets and along the sides of the auditorium (fig. 35). The cast of 900 featured 200 rabbis, 200 cantors, 400 actors and 100 musicians. Performers who donated their services included Paul Muni, Luther Adler, Edward G. Robinson and Jacob Ben Ami (who played the chief rabbi). A young and relatively unknown actor named Marlon Brando also appeared in the production.

The show began with the orchestra playing Yom Kippur music and a cantor singing the Kol Nidre, after which the chief rabbi emerged from between the two immense tablets and addressed the audience. "We are here to

Figure 35. Scene from the New York Production of *We Will Never Die*, 1943
(Courtesy Billy Rose Theatre Collection, New York Public Library, Astor, Lenox and Tilden Foundations)

say our prayers for the two million who have been killed in Europe," he began. "We are here to honor them and proclaim the victory of their dying. For in our Testament are written the words of Habakkuk, prophet of Israel, 'They shall never die.'"[19] After Ben Ami's introduction, twenty European rabbis entered holding aloft Torahs as the cantors recited the prayer of Shema Israel.

The pageant then moved through a series of narrated tableaux that depicted various events from Jewish history, including the recent Warsaw ghetto uprising. The final and most powerful segment of the show, "Remember Us," was a stark recitation of Nazi crimes by actors representing the Jewish dead:

Dead Man: The Germans came when we were at prayer. They tore the prayer shawls from our heads. Under whips and bayonets they made us use our prayer shawls as mops to clean out German latrines. We were all dead when the sun set.... Remember us.

Dead Woman: We were in Poland.... We hung from the windows and burned in basements.... We fill the waters of the Dnieper today with our bodies. And for a long time to come no one will be able to drink from the river because we are still there. And this, too, is held against us by the Germans—that we have poisoned their rivers with our dead bodies.... Remember us.[20]

After this chilling litany of German atrocities, a narrator came on-stage to conclude the program. "The massacre of Jews is not a Jewish situation," he began. "It is a problem that belongs to humanity. It is a challenge to the human soul."[21] The choir then sang a prayer as the actors representing the dead filed off-stage. Just before the cantors sang a prayer for the dead, the narrator offered his final remarks. "The Jews have only one voice left to raise among the governments of the world," he intoned solemnly. "It is the voice of prayer.... Perhaps the dying will hear it and find hope. Perhaps the Four Freedoms will hear it and find their tongue."[22]

Although the pageant was well received and focused public attention on the genocide in Europe, Hecht was discouraged that it did not raise more money for the cause of a Jewish homeland.[23] A year after the war, Hecht wrote another propaganda pageant, this time about Jewish attempts to oust the British from Palestine. Rose backed the show and helped produce it, but requested that his name not appear in the program credits. Although the production starred Paul Muni, Sidney Lumet and Marlon Brando, Hecht's *A Flag Is Born* failed to achieve the popularity of *We Will Never Die*. Wolcott Gibbs dismissed the piece as "a combination of dubious poetry and political oversimplification."[24] Although hardly a complete success from a theatrical standpoint, Hecht's efforts were much appreciated by the Jews fighting in Palestine. After Israel came into being as a nation, it named the first vessel in its navy the S.S. *Ben Hecht*.

Soon after *We Will Never Die* concluded its tour, Oscar Hammerstein came to Rose with an idea for a show. Hammerstein enjoyed a reputation among the songwriting community that far outweighed his limited commercial success. Rose shared the belief that, despite a series of failures in the 1930s, Hammerstein was one of the greats in his field. His recent work for *Oklahoma!* confirmed the faith that other lyricists and composers had placed in his talents. So it was with more than casual interest that Rose listened to Hammerstein's latest brainstorm.

The project involved a novel and (for 1943) daring reinterpretation of Georges Bizet's classic opera *Carmen* called *Carmen Jones*. Hammerstein proposed to set the action in present-day North Carolina and perform it with an all-black cast. In keeping with the wartime atmosphere, Carmen Jones worked in a local parachute factory. Don José became an AWOL soldier named Joe. Escamillo was a boxer named Husky Miller, and the bull ring became a boxing arena. Hammerstein retained all of Bizet's original music, but dropped the dull recitatives and changed the titles of the arias. The Toreador song, for example, became "Stan' Up an' Fight." The plot of the Mérimée novel (which was the basis for Bizet's libretto) was also kept intact, with Carmen murdered by Joe after she runs off to Chicago with Husky Miller.

Hammerstein had written the piece a year earlier but had failed to convince any producers of its viability. Most either shied away from his insistence on Negro performers or felt that it was impossible to assemble an entire cast of sufficiently talented black opera singers. Max Gordon had relinquished his option on the piece only a week before Hammerstein's initial discussion with Rose. The general opinion seemed to be that the project was unproducible.

Rose, however, displayed his usual propensity for ignoring a work's drawbacks and obstacles. He saw great potential in popularizing an already well-known opera and bringing a normally elitist theatrical form to a general audience. *Carmen Jones* seemed to suit perfectly his need to produce legitimate attractions while still retaining the elements of spectacle and popular appeal with which he was most comfortable. Rose was struck by Hammerstein's timely use of black performers. "We were supposed to be fighting for democracy," he later noted. "Why not make the point that it should include all the people?"[25]

Although Rose may well have been touched by nobler inclinations, he also saw that a group of unknown black performers could be hired for a fraction the salary of a noteworthy white cast. The two motives were perfect examples of his contradictory nature. Rose could produce holocaust pageants and all-black operas while haggling with chorus performers over an extra five dollars a week. It is some measure of his personality that he rarely found such instincts incompatible.

Rose agreed to produce *Carmen Jones* but was privately dubious that the show could be cast as written. Having learned of the project, *Variety* columnist Cecilia Ager put Rose and Hammerstein in touch with John Hammond, the noted jazz buff and producer who had brought such artists as Billie Holiday, Count Basie and Teddy Wilson to the attention of white audiences. Hammond was something of a legend in jazz circles and well respected as a record producer with impeccable taste and an ear for talent.

Hammond was so enthusiastic about the project that he offered to take on the job of casting the singing parts without remuneration. Rose, of course, agreed to this immediately, and in December 1942 Hammond embarked on a three-month tour of the country in search of black vocalists. He scoured black colleges and high schools and talked to music teachers, musicians and choir directors. Hammond auditioned thousands of young amateur and professional performers in cities and towns from coast to coast. His diligence led to some outstanding discoveries. Hammond's Carmen was Muriel Smith, a clerk in a Philadelphia camera store who had never before sung professionally. Joe was played by a timekeeper in the Philadelphia shipyard and Husky Miller by a New York City policeman; neither of the men had ever set foot on-stage. With the exception of one minor role, the cast was entirely composed of amateurs.

The production staff was already in place by the time casting was completed in the spring of 1943. Hassard Short was hired to direct and light the production, with Howard Bay designing the sets and Raoul Pène duBois designing the costumes. Perhaps Rose's greatest stroke in assembling his staff was the selection of Charles Friedman to direct the dramatic sequences and coach the amateur performers. Friedman, who had performed miracles in 1936 with the equally unseasoned cast of the International Ladies' Garment Workers' Union hit revue *Pins and Needles,* molded Hammond's inexperienced singers into a polished ensemble in only four months.

The show opened in Philadelphia on October 13 to the almost total acclaim of the press. Rose and Hammerstein felt the show was ready for New York, but they were unable to secure a theatre there. Needing ticket sales to meet ongoing costs and salaries, Rose made the unfortunate decision of bringing the production to Boston. The conservative audiences and the even more conservative music critics were unable to accept so radical a departure from Bizet, especially one with an entirely black cast. The show's cool reception was a severe blow after the heady notices in Philadelphia.

Rose and Hammerstein began to panic. Suppose Philadelphia had been an aberration? Perhaps *Carmen Jones* was not ready for New York. Even worse, perhaps New York was not ready for *Carmen Jones.* Rose, Hammerstein, Friedman, Short and the rest of the production staff met to consider their options. The show could hardly remain in Boston; but there was no place for it New York either. Without the publicity of a Broadway opening,

Carmen Jones could not wander the hinterlands indefinitely. There was talk of a major rewrite and the possibility of importing big-name black stars like Lena Horne and Bill Robinson. Spirits were low, and Rose decided to let the matter ride for another day before coming to a decision.

Several hours before Hammerstein, Rose and the others met again to decide the show's fate, a telegram arrived from J. J. Shubert. *Artists and Models,* which was playing at the Broadway Theatre, had closed unexpectedly. Shubert said the theatre would be available almost immediately. After another nervous staff meeting, Rose made the decision. "We've got a show and now we've got a theatre," he declared. "What the hell does Boston know? Let's go to New York."[26]

With the opening set for December 2, Rose went to work generating publicity. Having secured front-page coverage and lengthy feature pieces in Philadelphia and Boston, he became obsessed with doing the same in New York. Press agent Wolfe Kaufman, who had managed the show's publicity on the road, was doubtful that the same feat could be accomplished in the New York newspapers. Rose was determined, however, and he and Kaufman sat down and made a list of the various city editors, drama critics and newspaper publishers who might be willing to print a feature on an all-black show. Kaufman knew William Randolph Hearst, Jr. (the publisher of the *Journal* and the *Mirror*) from Hearst's days as a Chicago journalist. Trading on the Hearst family's penchant for things American, Rose wrote Hearst personally about how *Carmen Jones* (despite the Bizet score) was a truly "American opera" sung in red-blooded American English. Rose went on to say that he had invested $100,000 of his own money in a great battle against the Europeanized snobs who kept opera from the people. The pitch worked, and Hearst not only published several preshow features, but ran a three-column front page review of the opening.[27]

Both the New York and national critics praised the production extensively (fig. 36). George Freedley called it "far and away the best show in New York."[28] Robert Garland of the *New York Journal-American* hailed it as "a remarkable theatrical achievement on the part of Billy Rose," while Lewis Nichols of the *Times* said that it was "beautifully done...just call it wonderful."[29] But for Rose, the crowning compliment came from John Chapman who wrote a column comparing him to Ziegfeld and declared, "I cannot believe that even Ziegfeld would have had the imagination or the courage to produce Rose's *Carmen Jones.*"[30]

It did seem that Bizet would never be the same. *Variety* (and several other theatrical publications) suggested that *Carmen Jones* had shown up all "the hoary operas that go on season after season with little variation."[31] The general reaction on Broadway was aptly summed up when Deems Taylor remarked to Hammerstein that he had been to the Metropolitan Opera "to see *Carmen* in whiteface."[32]

Figure 36. Scenes from the 1943 New York Production of *Carmen Jones* *(Courtesy Billy Rose Theatre Collection, New York Public Library, Astor, Lenox and Tilden Foundations)*

Another measure of *Carmen Jones*'s popularity was demonstrated when Rose arranged a benefit for Hadassah a month after the show opened. Through an apparently unintentional slip-up, both the benefit tickets and the regular tickets for that evening were distributed, with the result that 3800 people appeared for 1900 seats. Wolfe Kaufman was stunned and called Rose who called the Shuberts who in turn called the riot police. Rose cooled things down by going to the theatre and telling the crowd that anyone without a seat would be given the choice of a ticket for another performance or a refund. He also took out advertisements in all the newspapers the following day to apologize for the mishap. Rose sent Lee Shubert the bills for both the ads and the additional ticket costs. Shubert was more than willing to pay, as the well-publicized fiasco had boosted *Carmen Jones*'s already outstanding attendance.[33]

Publicity stunts notwithstanding, the show was significant on a number of levels. *Carmen Jones* had managed to bring hitherto unknown black artists to the commercial stage at a time when segregation was an ironclad reality in all aspects of American life. Hammerstein and Rose showed that black talent was not limited to jazz and soft-shoe routines. *Carmen Jones*'s youthful and gifted cast had invigorated the opera and demonstrated that it could have a far more universal appeal than most Americans realized. Hammerstein's exuberant libretto proved, once again, that popular musical theatre and serious art could coexist in the same show.[34]

While *Carmen Jones* went on to a lengthy run and a successful tour, Rose turned his attention to other areas. Realizing that the show had nearly gone under for lack of an available New York theatre, Rose decided to buy one. He knew that the Hearsts, who now owned the Ziegfeld Theatre, were going to sell the building to cover the settlement costs of the senior William Randolph Hearst's estate. Since many of the late Hearst's holdings were in receivership, only sealed bids were being accepted, with court-appointed attorneys awarding the theatre to the highest bidder. After receiving inside information that Loew's, Inc. (which had run the theatre for the Hearsts as a movie house) had submitted a bid of $600,000, Rose topped the offer by $30,000. Despite strong suggestions from Loew's that he abandon his attempts to buy the theatre, Rose persisted and ultimately acquired the Ziegfeld. He then quickly bought out his partner, New Jersey politician Ben Marden, after having used Marden's Tammany Hall connections to clinch the deal. Several weeks after the sale, Loew's offered to buy the theatre from Rose for $800,000. At the time of Rose's death in 1966, the Ziegfeld was sold to the Fisher brothers for $18,000,000.[35]

Having obtained the theatre, Rose was now determined to complete his assumption of Ziegfeld's mantle by producing a revue of lavish and unprecedented proportions. Some years earlier, Rose had read Gilbert

Seldes's 1924 book *The Seven Lively Arts*, which critically examined such popular entertainments as vaudeville, motion pictures and jazz. Seldes's essays gave Rose an idea for a show that combined all the arts in one mammoth production along the lines of Casa Mañana's ill-fated *The Big Show*, only on a far grander scale. Rose boasted to Lucius Beebe that the show would not contain "an ounce of significance... or a trace of moral purpose.... It's the last word in complete escapism... a grab-bag of fun."[36]

It was indeed a grab bag, and a famous one at that. Rose hired Cole Porter to do the music and Igor Stravinsky to compose a ballet score for the second act. Anton Dolin and Alicia Markova were cast to dance the Stravinsky piece with a thirty-member corps de ballet. Bert Lahr and Beatrice Lillie were the principal comic stars, accompanied by Doc Rockwell, Dolores Gray, and Benny Goodman, who played several classical clarinet pieces as well as some contemporary swing numbers. George S. Kaufman and Moss Hart wrote the sketches, with Ben Hecht providing monologue material for Doc Rockwell. Norman Bel Geddes designed the scenery, Philip Loeb directed the sketches, and Hassard Short lit and staged the production.

Seven Lively Arts was reminiscent of Rose's first revues, *Sweet and Low* and *Crazy Quilt*, in its hodgepodge construction and pell-mell assemblage of stars. But where the earlier shows were relatively humble in scale and scope, *Seven Lively Arts* was decidedly overblown, especially for a nation in the middle of a world war.[37]

Rose's approach with *Seven Lively Arts* was the exact opposite of the tack he took with *Carmen Jones*. Whereas the earlier show had relied on unknown performers and an exceptional script, *Seven Lively Arts* featured a surfeit of stars in a thoroughly mediocre and shopworn vehicle. In his zeal to surpass Ziegfeld, Rose overlooked the vital components of spontaneity and freshness central to any comic enterprise. Rose's show was so top-heavy with stars and big-name collaborators that it never stood a chance of coalescing as a production. As he had in *Clash by Night*, Rose again made the mistake of employing performers with egos as great as his own. Only this time, instead of just the singularly irascible Tallulah Bankhead, he had a half dozen temperamental luminaries with whom to contend.

Problems cropped up before rehearsals even began. Beatrice Lillie expressed dissatisfaction with the songs written for her by Cole Porter and requested to bring some material with her from London. Porter objected strenuously to this; his contract stated that other composers' material could only be included with his permission. Already in the position of sharing the bill with Stravinsky, Porter was in no mood to compromise. Rose somehow managed to smooth over the dispute, with Lillie ultimately performing Porter's material and two of her own selections.

Stravinsky was also perturbed when his "Scènes de Ballet" number was reduced to a mere fifteen minutes. On top of this, Rose had the audacity to suggest that the material be reorchestrated, and telegraphed Stravinsky:

> YOUR MUSIC GREAT SUCCESS **STOP** COULD BE SENSATIONAL SUCCESS IF YOU WOULD AUTHORIZE ROBERT RUSSELL BENNETT RETOUCH ORCHESTRATION **STOP** BENNETT ORCHESTRATES EVEN THE WORKS OF COLE PORTER.

Stravinsky replied calmly, "SATISFIED WITH GREAT SUCCESS."[38]

Bert Lahr was also unhappy and felt that his material was decidedly substandard. He was particularly opposed to the patter in a song Cole Porter wrote for him called "Dainty Quainty Me":

> When people talk about those columnists, such as
> Walter Winchell, Ed Sullivan, Westbrook Pegler...
> And that frightfully vulgar girl they call "ELSA,"
> I take BROMO SELTZA.
>
> When one mentions Martha Raye, Carmen Miranda,...
> Sir Cedric Hardwicke and other stars of the CINEMA,
> I have to take an ENEMA.[39]

Lahr also refused to go along with a Moss Hart sketch in which an English officer lectures his men on the evils of fraternization with women. He becomes thoroughly aroused during the scene and is finally cooled down with a bucket of water. Already less than enthusiastic about the show, Lahr would have nothing to do with the sketch. "I didn't want to get drenched every day. It wasn't worth it."[40] He did convince Cole Porter to write an amusing send-up of the many drinking songs in the Shubert musicals of the twenties. Backed up by a husky-voiced male chorus, Lahr appeared in an admiral's uniform and got progressively drunker as he toasted several well-worn Shubert successes:

> Drink to *The Student Prince* that show sublime,
> And don't forget Jeanette in *Apple Blossom Time*.
> Drink to Nelson Eddy, before you faint,
> And here's to J. J. Shubert, our patron saint.[41]

Although she too had objected to some of Porter's compositions, Beatrice Lillie came off somewhat better than Lahr and was given the show's only noteworthy song, "Ev'ry Time We Say Goodbye." It was the only number from the Porter score that survived *Seven Lively Arts* to become a hit on its own. Lillie also had several amusing scenes with Lahr, including "Fragonard," a satire of eighteenth-century manners. Clad in an excessively

134   The War and After

Figure 37. Beatrice Lillie and Bert Lahr in "Fragonard" from the New York Production of *Seven Lively Arts*
(Courtesy Billy Rose Theatre Collection, New York Public Library, Astor, Lenox and Tilden Foundations)

pink and frilly dress, Lillie glided back and forth in a garlanded swing while Lahr twittered about in matching pink tights (fig. 37).

Despite its complex and unwieldy configuration, the show had only a week's exposure out of town before arriving in New York. Although he was familiar with the problems of excessive scenery from his first out-of-town opening fourteen years earlier (with *Corned Beef and Roses,* see chapter 1), Rose seemed unperturbed by the fact that ten railroad cars were required to move the sets and costumes to Philadelphia. On November 24, 1944 the show that *Billboard* described as "one of the most lavish and pretentious revues ever to grace a row of footlights" opened at the Forrest Theatre.[42] While the cumbersome production had its problems, *Billboard* noted that "its shortcomings were entirely lost in the grandeur and pretentiousness of the production.... It is not just big, beautiful and dumb.... It has much more vitality than the Ziegfeld *Follies* series and averages more humor than most of them too."[43]

Although the Philadelphia reviewers were quick to point out that Lahr and Lillie were much more engaging than their show, Rose was anxious to bring *Seven Lively Arts* to New York. He had used rumors of excessive ticket scalping to generate an incredible advance sale on Broadway. Three days before the Philadelphia opening, Rose took out newspaper advertisements denying that the show was being presold: "You can bet your bottom dollar that I'm keeping faith with Mr. John Q. Public," the blurb began. "The fancypants set has never been important in my scheme of things. The money to buy the Ziegfeld Theatre came from the 11,000,000 who saw the *Aquacade*. They're my people and I want to be their boy."[44]

Rose's Barnumesque proclamation aside, the New York opening of *Seven Lively Arts* was anything but proletarian. The $24 ticket price was the highest yet charged for a Broadway premiere and included champagne at intermission. Rose had lavishly redecorated the Ziegfeld with the assistance of the late impresario's widow Billie Burke, who accompanied Rose and Eleanor Holm to the opening. The lobby featured surreal anatomical interpretations of seven decidedly lively arts by Salvador Dali, painted especially for the occasion.[45]

For a nation at war, it was a strange and often vulgar spectacle. "The gangways seethed with the names that made news hoisting fire pails of champagne at the expense of the management," wrote Lucius Beebe. "The limousine line stretched from the theater's blindingly lighted marquee all the way to Central Park.... [No] other social clambake... has in recent years brought out such an undulant red carpet of chinchilla and boiled shirts."[46]

The opulence in the audience was equaled by the sprawling extravagance on-stage. *Time* commented that the show was "less like the seven lively arts than like seven luxury hotels."[47] Lewis Nichols of the *New York Times* concurred. "It is big and rambling and sometimes it is top-heavy... but as a Broadway show it is right in the groove."[48] The *Tribune* agreed, calling *Seven Lively Arts* "both inspired and ordinary."[49] The show's odd mixture of the genuinely entertaining with the patently banal was exemplified in the first act finale, entitled "Billy Rose Buys the Metropolitan Opera House." It was a curious collection of snippets from previous Rose productions interspersed with some inspired playing by Benny Goodman. *Variety* maintained that the segment should have been retitled "Glorifying the American Rose." Most of the other production numbers received an equally tepid response. Despite commendable performances by Dolin and Markova, Stravinsky's ballet was described in *Billboard* as "far from startling."[50] Robert Garland of the *Journal* offered perhaps the most succinct summation. "Somewhere in *Seven Lively Arts* a show of shows is buried. Last night it didn't happen to be forthcoming."[51]

Despite the lukewarm reviews, Rose managed to keep the show running for 183 performances, due largely to the tremendous advance sale. He was probably the only person associated with the show who wanted it kept alive. Lillie was angered by Rose's habit of sending notes on her performance to her dressing room each night. After she threatened to quit, Rose ran quarter-page advertisements in the major papers extolling her under the heading "I Tip My Hat to Beatrice Lillie." Lahr was offended by this and threatened to take out his own signed advertisement labeled: "I Tip My Hat to [producer] Mike Todd." The show closed before Lahr could follow through with his plan.[52] Rose later claimed that he would never again work "with big stars... please, give me the elephants, the yaks and the giraffes."[53]

The nine years between *Seven Lively Arts* and Rose's next Broadway show were both financially successful and personally agonizing. The Ziegfeld Theatre prospered, and the Diamond Horseshoe remained immensely popular until its closing in 1951 (see chapter 5). At the suggestion of Bell Syndicate editor John Wheeler, Rose also undertook a career as a columnist and wrote the syndicated "Pitching Horseshoes" series from 1947 to 1950. He collected many of these breezy pronouncements in *Wine, Women and Words,* a rambling autobiographical volume published in 1949.[54] As with other Rose projects, the column's success and wide distribution owed much to its author's tireless promotion. Typical of Rose's zeal was his conversation with the editor of a small-town paper in Oklahoma:

"This is Billy Rose."
"Billy Rose? *The* Billy Rose?"
"Yeah, Billy. I want you to buy my column."
"I can't afford your column."
"Can you afford fifty cents a week?"
"Sure."
"Okay, you got the column. You'll have it by air in a few hours."[55]

Rose's personal drum beating was muted significantly by his messy four-year divorce from Eleanor Holm. The press broadsides that accompanied his abandonment of Fanny Brice were nothing compared to the deluge of tawdry notices generated by what became known as the "War of the Roses." The spectacular trial was precipitated by Rose's indiscreet affair with actress Joyce Matthews. When Rose refused to divorce Holm and marry her, Matthews locked herself in his Ziegfeld Theatre office and slit her wrists. This garish incident was just a prelude to the vicious battle that ensued when Holm filed for divorce. By the time a settlement was announced in January 1954, Rose had spent well over a million dollars in legal fees and court costs. In addition, he paid Holm $200,000 in cash and $30,000 a month in alimony.[56]

Anxious to see his name mentioned in some other context than the lurid accounts of his divorce, Rose began to search for a new project. When his friend, writer Paul Osborne, suggested that Rose take a look at a new play by

Ruth and Augustus Goetz, he was only too happy to oblige. The Goetzes, who had previously written the successful Broadway adaptation of Henry James's *The Heiress,* had just finished their stage version of André Gide's 1902 novel, *The Immoralist.*

Gide's book was a frank (and for its day, daring) attempt to chronicle the conflicts brought about by his marriage and avowed homosexuality. The plot concerns a young homosexual archaeologist who, against his better judgment, marries a girl from his hometown in France and embarks with her on a field trip to Tunisia. He has trouble consummating the marriage and subsequently takes up with a young Arab boy, causing his wife to begin drinking. Although Gide did not live to see his work on-stage, he had discussed the project with the Goetzes and had given them complete authority to adapt the work as they saw fit.

Knowing Rose's penchant for spectacle, the Goetzes were afraid that the play's North African setting might prompt him (in Augustus Goetz's words) "to use up some of those elephants he's had in storage."[57] They were, in fact, pleasantly surprised at Rose's reaction to the script. "The show needs a simple, quiet production," Rose told them. "All you want onstage is feeling—the deepest, purest emotion you can get."[58] Rose knew that the subject matter was dangerous territory, but decided to take a chance and produce the play himself. "Had someone asked me to buy a 2 percent interest in it, I would have turned it down as an uneasy risk," he wrote shortly before the New York opening. "To produce this distinguished 100-1 shot on my own, however, made some sort of upside-down sense."[59]

Although Rose probably had no great interest in homosexuality as a social issue, the Goetzes sensed that he was drawn to the play by the quality of its emotional message. "One of the reasons Billy had so much feeling for the play," they wrote, "is that he realizes that loneliness is a universal problem.... Billy has always done shows aimed to appeal to a vast number of people, and we learned that the same thing that makes one able to intrigue a mass audience helps him when he is going after a special audience."[60]

Rose selected Herman Shumlin to direct the show, and cast Louis Jourdan as the archaeologist and Geraldine Page as his wife. The cast also included a young James Dean as Jourdan's Arab lover. Rehearsals were smooth as Rose productions went, although Shumlin left after several weeks of arguments with the Goetzes over the script. He was replaced by Daniel Mann, who later directed Elizabeth Taylor in the Oscar-winning film *Butterfield 8.* Throughout the show's preparation, Rose was a remarkable model of restraint. "His taste has been good, his suggestions discreet and his judgement quick," the Goetzes noted.

Rose treated the show with kid gloves partly because he knew that it represented his last production on Broadway. And although *Variety* said that

Figure 38. Geraldine Page and Louis Jourdan in the 1954 New York Production of *The Immoralist*
(Courtesy Billy Rose Theatre Collection, New York Public Library, Astor, Lenox and Tilden Foundations)

The Immoralist was "fine theatre but uncertain box office," the show proved a reasonable success on its arrival at the Royale Theatre on February 8, 1954 (fig. 38).[61] Brooks Atkinson called *The Immoralist* "an admirable piece of work that retains the integrity of Gide and does credit to the good taste of the Goetzes.... The tragedy is austere, crushing and genuine."[62]

Rose kept the show profitable by offering all unsold balcony seats for ninety-nine cents apiece on a first-come, first-served basis. Determined to end his producing activities on a positive note, Rose closed *The Immoralist* while it was still grossing more than $20,000 a week. "Your play is my swan song as a producer," he told the Goetzes, so I'm going to close it while it's still making money. Forgive me for wanting to wind up my Broadway career with the ledger in the black."[63]

Although *The Immoralist* did indeed mark the end of his career as a Broadway producer, Rose was hardly out of the public eye. The following year, he became involved in a dispute with his old nemesis Robert Moses.

Moses was outraged when Rose suggested to reporters that Central Park be turned into an amusement park along the lines of Copenhagen's Tivoli Gardens. "As long as I'm around New York, Central Park will not be turned into a nightclub," Moses responded in typical fashion; "Billy Rose is taking in entirely too much territory."[64] Fortunately for Moses and New York, Rose soon dropped the idea.

The same year, however, he came close to realizing an equally grandiose scheme: the construction of a permanent world's fair on top of Penn Station. The hundred-million-dollar project proposed a seven-million-square-foot Palace of Progress and an equally outsized hotel and office complex atop a completely rebuilt train terminal. Detailed plans for the colossal structure were released by the Zeckendorf Co. (contractors for the United Nations complex), but financing proved too difficult to obtain and the project was abandoned.[65]

Still, Rose never lost his penchant for entertainment on a grand scale. Perhaps the most gargantuan idea was his proposal in 1956 of an outdoor air spectacle called, appropriately enough, *Aircade*. Rose envisioned staging a huge "musical in the sky" at racetracks before audiences of more than 100,000. The show would feature precision airplane stunts to music provided by two orchestras housed in stationary dirigibles. Although his stamina may have failed him in later years, Rose's imagination remained as active as ever.

In 1958, Rose acquired the National Theatre on Forty-first Street and renamed it the Billy Rose. The purchase led to one last involvement with a Broadway show. In 1962, two young producers, David Barr and Clinton Wilder, brought Rose the first full-length play by a recently acclaimed off-Broadway playwright named Edward Albee. Seeing the work's potential, Rose became a silent partner and watched *Who's Afraid of Virginia Woolf?* become one of his second theatre's biggest hits. By this time, however, he was far more involved in lucrative stock market transactions than in the fare presented at his theatres. Except for the well-publicized donation of his sculpture collection to Israel, Rose tried to stay out of the limelight.

One of Rose's last public performances was a radio broadcast from the Plaza Hotel for the Tex McCrary program on July 9, 1965. He tried, in his own self-caricaturing style, to sum up his life. "Good, bad, big or little, I have done about one hundred shows in my life," he declared, "and I think I am understating that in the past thirty years I sold substantially more than one hundred million tickets to the public." When asked to describe himself, Rose paused and his tone changed.

> To be very honest about it, I don't quite know who I am. I have had eleven reasonably successful careers in my crazy mixed-up life. I can only refer to myself as my mother's son. I am Billy Rose with all the good it stands for, with all the bad it stands for.... I cannot compare myself to anybody because I am a little more mixed-up than anybody I can think of."[66]

Seven months and one day later, on February 10, 1966, Billy Rose died of pneumonia at a nursing home in Jamaica.

Billy Rose's mark on the theatre of his day was considerable, but in the end even he realized that contemporary trends were passing him by. Writing of Ziegfeld and the great impresarios of his generation, Rose noted that "today, the cape and beaver collar have been replaced by banker's grey."[67] Theatre had always been a business, but now it was big business and the flamboyant risk-takers of Billy Rose's day no longer had a place in it. The style, methods and content of the commercial theatre had changed, although not perhaps as much as some people imagined in the late 1960s.

Divining the lasting influence of Billy Rose on American theatre is as elusive a task as assessing the man himself. In many respects, Rose's legacy is not to be found in any of his productions; the raw materials he used— vaudeville, circus, burlesque, spectacle and musical comedy—were there when he found them and remained more or less the same when he left. Rather, it was his eclectic blending of these previously distinct traditions and methods that had a genuine impact on the theatre that came after him.[68]

Rose was, in the most elementary sense of the word, a showman, a man whose uncanny sense of the theatrical was larger than the theatre itself. "That man is the most extraordinary showman in America," Lillian Gish once said. "We have only three real showmen in our theatre today—Billy Rose, Orson Welles and José Ferrer. It is a self-evident talent, an instinct, call it what you will."[69] "One of the secrets of Rose's success," *Time* observed, "is that whatever he produces makes a good story long before it makes a good show."[70] This ability to project both his theatrical activities and his personality into the public consciousness was one of Rose's most remarkable talents.

This same propensity for manipulation and self-aggrandizement also made him one of the most hated men in twentieth-century American theatre. Clifford Odets saw Rose's many contradictions as indicative of America's character as a nation. "The problem of Billy Rose is the problem of the U.S.A.... What's good about him is American and what's bad about him is American. He wasn't made by another country."[71] Ben Hecht concurred, and noted that one of Rose's few genuine affections was for America, particularly the city of New York. "Fame lay hidden in it, to be gone after with pick and shovel," Hecht wrote in his autobiography. "Billy had a residence and an office, but his true home was the cacophonic street and the café."[72]

Rose was driven by New York's rhythms. He needed the city and drew his energy from it. "When I walk down Broadway with Billy Rose," Hecht wrote, "I become aware of its lights... as if I hadn't quite marked them before. The

Broadway that is always a dusty, half-slatternly amusement park in my eyes, changes for me as Billy looks at it."[73] Rose loved American popular entertainment not only because he believed in the "Barnum and Bailey world" of his songs and shows, but, more important, because he lived in it. Like New York itself, Billy Rose was his own best performance.

Notes

Chapter 1

1. Billy Rose, *Wine, Women and Words* (New York: Simon and Schuster, 1946), p. 9.
2. Earl Conrad, *Manhattan Primitive* (New York: World Publishing, 1968), p. 15.
3. Polly Rose Gottlieb, *The Nine Lives of Billy Rose* (New York: Crown Publishers, 1968), p. 69.
4. Conrad, p. 19.
5. Gottlieb, p. 71.
6. Rose, p. 10.
7. Conrad, pp. 23–26.
8. Rose, p. 10.
9. Gottlieb, p. 75.
10. Rose, p. 10.
11. Conrad, pp. 47–48.
12. Ibid.
13. Conrad, p. 63
14. Ibid., p. 62.
15. Billy Rose, Marty Bloom and Ernest Breuer, "Does the Spearmint Lose Its Flavor (on the Bedpost Overnight?)," Mills Music, 1924.
16. Rudi Blesh and Harriet Janis, *They All Played Ragtime* (New York: Oak Publications, 1966), pp. 38–40.
17. Ibid.
18. Conrad, p. 67.
19. Ibid.
20. Rose, p. 11.
21. Gottlieb, p. 79.

22. Conrad, p. 69.
23. Rose, p. 11.
24. Conrad, p. 70.
25. Rose, p. 15.
26. Rose, p. 12.
27. Gottlieb, p. 81.
28. Rose, p. 12.
29. Gilbert Seldes, "Stage-Door Johnny, Pro-Tem," *Esquire*, September 1934, p. 137.
30. Rose, p. 12.
31. Gottlieb, p. 83.
32. Rose, p. 13.
33. Seldes, p. 154.

Chapter 2

1. Thomas H. Gressler, "John Murray Anderson: Director of Revues" (Ph.D. dissertation, Kent State University, 1973), p. 18.
2. *Encyclopedia Britannica* (Chicago: Encyclopedia Britannica, Inc., 1970), XIX, pp. 248-49.
3. Wolcott Gibbs, "A Little Something for Almost Everybody," *The New Yorker*, December 19, 1953, p. 75.
4. Charles B. Cochran, "The Revue as an Art Form," *Forthnightly Review*, September 1925, pp. 359-61. Cochran's definition is particularly prescient in Rose's case since Rose's first revue borrowed almost entirely the Venetian Box sequence from Cochran's London revue.
5. Conrad, p. 86.
6. *New York Times*, November 30, 1930.
7. Jo Mielziner, renderings and elevations for *Sweet and Low*, September 1930, Mielziner Collection, Box 11, New York Public Library at Lincoln Center, New York, New York.
8. *New York Morning Telegram*, October 13, 1930.
9. *Variety*, October 22, 1930.
10. Ibid.
11. Ibid.
12. *Philadelphia Enquirer*, October 15, 1930.
13. *Variety*, October 22, 1930; *New York Times*, November 18, 1930.
14. *New York Daily News*, October 29, 1930.
15. David Freedman, *New York Herald Tribune*, December 2, 1930.
16. *New York Times*, November 18, 1930.
17. *New York World*, November 18, 1930.

Notes for Chapter 2   145

18. *Sweet and Low,* miscellaneous sides, Billy Rose Collection, Box 5, folder 3, New York Public Library at Lincoln Center, New York, New York.

19. Rose blamed excessive scenery expense and slow business prior to the first of the year. Richard Maney claimed that much of the weekly gross went directly into Rose's pocket and that investors were presented with bogus figures to make the show look like a loser.

20. Program, *Crazy Quilt,* Billy Rose Collection.

21. Newspaper advertisement for *Crazy Quilt,* May 1930, Billy Rose Collection.

22. Conrad, pp. 88-89.

23. Rose, p. 14.

24. Ibid.

25. John Murray Anderson, *Out without My Rubbers* (New York: Library Publishers, 1953), p. 145.

26. Flyer for *Crazy Quilt,* Billy Rose Collection, Box 3, folder 1.

27. Anderson, p. 145.

28. Ben Hecht and Gene Fowler, *The Great Magoo,* frontispiece of original typescript, Billy Rose Theatre Collection, New York Public Library at Lincoln Center, New York, New York.

29. Richard Maney, *Fanfare: The Confessions of a Press Agent* (New York: Harper & Brothers, 1957), p. 113.

30. Ibid.

31. Brooks Atkinson, review of *The Great Magoo, New York Times,* December 3, 1932.

32. Robert Garland, *New York World Telegram,* December 3, 1932.

33. Billy Rose, E. Y. Harburg and Harold Arlen, "It's Only a Paper Moon," Harms, Inc., 1933.

34. Gottlieb, p. 90.

35. Billy Rose, quoted by A. J. Liebling in "Master of His Own House," *New York World Telegram,* May 19, 1934.

36. Billy Rose, quoted by Lucius Beebe in "Billy Rose Revives a Tradition But Isn't 'Over-Elegant' about It," *New York Herald Tribune,* January 18, 1934.

37. *Family Circle,* March 30, 1934.

38. Casino de Paree table card, Billy Rose Collection, Box 3, folder 4.

39. *Family Circle,* March 30, 1934.

40. Beebe, "Billy Rose Revives a Tradition."

41. Ibid.

42. Billy Rose, Ben Hecht, Ballard MacDonald and Vernon Duke, "Small Timers," manuscript for comedy routine, Billy Rose Collection, Box 5, folder 8.

43. Lyrics and music for both songs by Billy Rose, Jack Murray and Phil Baxter. From Casino de Paree program, Billy Rose Collection, Box 2, folder 1.

44. George Jean Nathan, column in *Judge,* 1933, n.d. From scrapbook in Billy Rose Collection.
45. Rose, p. 15.
46. Billy Rose, quoted by Liebling.

Chapter 3

1. Tommy ("Three Finger Brown") Lucchese, quoted by Billy Rose in "Pitching Horseshoes," *New York Daily News,* September 8, 1947.
2. Conrad, p. 78.
3. Thirty years later when Rose was recovering from surgery in a Houston hospital, he got a call from Tommy ("Three Finger Brown") Lucchese. The mobster told him, "We want you to get well. Remember Billy, we're responsible for you."
4. Maney, p. 155.
5. Maurice Zolotow, *Billy Rose of Broadway,* unpublished manuscript, 1945, p. 338, Billy Rose Collection.
6. Billy Rose, quoted by Richard Maney in "Rose Plans a Circus without Animals," *New York Herald Tribune,* August 19, 1934.
7. Ibid.
8. Zolotow, p. 340.
9. Maney, p. 153.
10. "Now It Can Be Told," *New York Times,* September 22, 1935.
11. Various letters offering animal acts for *Jumbo,* Billy Rose Collection, Box 5, folder 2.
12. *Brooklyn Daily Eagle,* February 18, 1935.
13. Gottlieb, p. 97.
14. Maney, p. 156. As this episode indicates, Rose's craving for publicity was often costly.
15. "Now It Can Be Told."
16. *New York Herald Tribune,* May 12, 1935.
17. The Whitneys were not Rose's only angels. Baruch and Swope contributed $15,000 each to their old stenographer's show.
18. Anderson, p. 146.
19. Conrad, p. 103.
20. *New York Herald Tribune,* April 7, 1935.
21. *Jumbo* press release, September 1935, Billy Rose Theatre Collection, Box 4, folder 3.
22. Draft of *Jumbo* contract, Actors' Equity Theatre Collection, Robert F. Wagner Labor Archives, New York, New York, uncatalogued contracts and correspondence.
23. The union also realized that several months of rehearsal pay for a cast of over two hundred would bankrupt the show before it opened.
24. Correspondence of Frank Gilmore, Actors' Equity Theatre Collection.

25. Anderson, p. 148.
26. Ibid.
27. *New York Herald Tribune,* October 23, 1935.
28. Ibid.
29. Maney, p. 157.
30. Ibid.
31. Maney, p. 157.
32. Zolotow, p. 375.
33. Ibid.
34. Fanny Brice, quoted by Zolotow, p. 377.
35. Ibid.
36. Anderson, p. 149.
37. Rose, p. 16.
38. Partial script, *Jumbo,* Billy Rose Theatre Collection, Box 5, folder 3.
39. *Jumbo* souvenir program, Billy Rose Theatre Collection. The two circus owners were played by Arthur Sinclair (Considine) and W. J. McCarthy (Mulligan).
40. *Jumbo* program, Billy Rose Theatre Collection.
41. Zolotow, pp. 381–82.
42. *Variety,* November 27, 1935.
43. Ibid.
44. Photographs of *Jumbo,* Billy Rose Theatre Collection.
45. Zolotow, p. 390.
46. Percy Hammond, *New York Herald Tribune,* November 18, 1935.
47. Brooks Atkinson, *New York Times,* November 18, 1935.
48. Gilbert Gabriel, *New York American,* November 18, 1935.
49. Eugene Burr, *Billboard,* November 30, 1935.
50. Legal brief summarizing the Carroll claim. Billy Rose Theatre Collection, Box 6, folder 3.
51. Financial records, Fort Worth Centennial, Billy Rose Theatre Collection, Box 1, folder 1.
52. Based on Rose's expense figures, the seating capacity of the Hippodrome, and the schedule of published ticket prices.

Chapter 4

1. Zolotow, p. 375.
2. Ibid.
3. Zolotow, p. 378.

4. Billy Rose, telegram to Richard Maney, March 3, 1936, Billy Rose Theatre Collection, Box 4, folder 3.
5. Billy Rose, notes for "Pitching Horseshoes," 1947, Billy Rose Theatre Collection.
6. Zolotow, p. 373.
7. Zolotow, p. 377
8. Zolotow, p. 368.
9. Chicago Historical Society, Chicago, Illinois, clippings and press releases, Century of Progress Exposition, 1933.
10. Ibid.
11. Museum of Science and Industry, Chicago, Illinois, advertisement in *Fair Weekly,* August 12, 1933.
12. Rose had given thought to expositions prior to his chance meeting with Le Maire. In February 1936, over a month before the Fort Worth job materialized, Rose proposed a World's Fair on Wheels that would tour the country under canvas.
13. Zolotow, p. 377.
14. Souvenir program, Fort Worth Centennial, 1936, Billy Rose Theatre Collection.
15. Ibid.
16. *Today,* November 7, 1936.
17. Ibid.
18. *Fort Worth Press,* June 14, 1936.
19. Production notes, Fort Worth Centennial, Billy Rose Theatre Collection.
20. *New York Sun,* April 16, 1936.
21. Program for *Jumbo,* Fort Worth production, Billy Rose Theatre Collection.
22. Anderson, p. 163.
23. Zolotow, p. 380.
24. *New York Post,* April 22, 1936.
25. Anderson, p. 165.
26. Casa Mañana souvenir program, Billy Rose Theatre Collection.
27. "You're in Paree," words by Billy Rose, music by Dana Suesse, manuscript copy of lyrics for Fort Worth Centennial, 1936, Billy Rose Theatre Collection.
28. Photographs of Casa Mañana Revue, 1936, courtesy *Fort Worth Star-Telegram.*
29. "It Happened in Chicago," words by Billy Rose, music by Dana Suesse, manuscript copy of lyrics for Fort Worth Centennial, 1936, Billy Rose Theatre Collection.
30. *Fort Worth Star-Telegram,* July 20, 1936.
31. In best Fort Worth fashion, the finale was accompanied by much whooping and hollering. On opening night, many cowboy hats were tossed into the water as the gondolas went by.
32. Damon Runyon, *New York American,* July 21, 1936.

Notes for Chapter 5 149

33. Maney, p. 175.
34. Rose, p. 21.
35. Fort Worth Frontier Fiesta, souvenir program, 1937, Billy Rose Theatre Collection. The scenes were loosely adapted from the plots of *Gone with the Wind* by Margaret Mitchell, *Lost Horizon* by James Hilton, *Wake Up and Live* by Dorothea Brande, and *It Can't Happen Here* by Sinclair Lewis.
36. Ibid.
37. "It Can't Happen Here," words by Billy Rose, music by Dana Suesse, manuscript copy of lyrics for Fort Worth Frontier Fiesta, 1937, Billy Rose Theatre Collection.
38. Paul Whiteman, quoted in the *New York Herald Tribune,* July 19, 1936.
39. Billy Rose, quoted in the *New York World Telegram,* October 10, 1936.
40. Billy Rose, telegram to Richard Maney, January 8, 1937, Billy Rose Theatre Collection.

Chapter 5

1. Souvenir guide, Great Lakes Exposition, 1936, p. 3.
2. Ibid. The promise of large-scale urban improvements was by this time a popular ploy of exposition promoters anxious to obtain public funds.
3. *Cleveland Plain Dealer,* n.d., 1936.
4. Souvenir guide, Great Lakes Exposition, 1936, pp. 8–11.
5. Souvenir guide, Great Lakes Exposition, 1936, p. 14.
6. Zolotow, p. 393.
7. Rose, p. 25.
8. Oscar Brockett, *History of the Theatre* (Boston: Allyn and Bacon, 1977), p. 60.
9. Conrad, p. 112.
10. Ibid.
11. Westbrook Pegler, *New York Post,* June 9, 1936.
12. Conrad, p. 114.
13. Conrad, p. 112
14. Balance sheet for Great Lakes Exposition amusements, 1937, Billy Rose Theatre Collection.
15. Ibid.
16. Zolotow, pp. 402-3.
17. *Aquacade* program, Great Lakes Exposition, 1937, p. 7
18. Anderson, p. 176.
19. *Aquacade* program, Great Lakes Exposition, 1937, p. 7.
20. Anderson, p. 177.
21. Since the 1937 Fort Worth and Cleveland productions overlapped and shared the same design and production staffs, there was a good deal of intrashow borrowing.

22. Script for Cleveland *Aquacade*, 1937, Billy Rose Theatre Collection
23. Ibid.
24. Mrs. E. L. Wilson, interviewed in San Francisco, California, November 20, 1984. Mrs. Wilson saw both the Cleveland and San Francisco *Aquacades*.
25. Despite poor rehearsal conditions, Rose's luck with the weather improved dramatically during the run of the show. According to exposition records, only three performances were rained out.
26. Script for Cleveland *Aquacade*, 1937, Billy Rose Theatre Collection.
27. Ibid.
28. "It Can't Happen Here," lyrics by Billy Rose, music by Dana Suesse; script for Cleveland *Aquacade*, 1937, Billy Rose Theatre Collection.
29. Photographs, Cleveland *Aquacade*, 1937, Billy Rose Theatre Collection.
30. Zolotow, p. 408.
31. Billy Rose, notes for "Pitching Horseshoes," Billy Rose Theatre Collection.

Chapter 6

1. Zolotow, p. 409.
2. *New York Daily Mirror*, November 12, 1937.
3. Zolotow, p. 408.
4. World's fair materials, 1939, New York Public Library.
5. Ibid.
6. Zolotow, p. 416.
7. *Time*, May 1, 1939, p. 72. Conflict-of-interest questions arose when Coty was awarded a prominently located pavilion at the fair.
8. For a more detailed discussion of the planning and development of the 1939 Fair, see chapter 6.
9. Brochure for Casa Mañana, 1938, Billy Rose Theatre Collection.
10. Advertisement for Casa Mañana, Billy Rose Theatre Collection.
11. Ibid.
12. *New Brunswick Home News*, January 10, 1938. For a discussion of Rose's approach to girlie shows, see chapter 4. His use of young and inexperienced chorus girls also enabled him to avoid paying union scale. Rose's firing of a performer for attempting to unionize the chorus at Casa Mañana ultimately led to a waiters' strike that closed the club in 1939.
13. Gottlieb, p. 114.
14. Ibid.
15. Rose later claimed the opening was delayed so that Shaw could grow a Whalen-like moustache. A more likely reason for the postponement was the need for additional rehearsal time.

16. Prompt script for *Let's Play Fair* by Billy Rose; "World's Fair Song," lyrics by Billy Rose, music by Dana Suesse, 1938, Billy Rose Theatre Collection. Such whimsical creations as the song describes were not uncommon at world's fairs. The 1929 Wembley Exposition had a diorama of the Prince of Wales and the Royal Family made entirely of mutton fat.
17. Prompt script for *Let's Play Fair* by Billy Rose, 1938, Billy Rose Theatre Collection.
18. Ibid.
19. "Throw a Little Party," lyrics by Billy Rose, music by Dana Suesse, 1938, Billy Rose Theatre Collection.
20. "Give Them Girls," lyrics by Billy Rose, music by Dana Suesse, 1938, Billy Rose Theatre Collection.
21. *New York Herald Tribune,* January 19, 1938.
22. This should not be confused with the female anatomical model displayed at the New York World's Fair and now housed in the American Museum of Natural History.
23. "New York on Parade," lyrics by Billy Rose, music by Dana Suesse, 1938, Billy Rose Theatre Collection.
24. Contract between New York World's Fair and Billy Rose, 1938, Billy Rose Theatre Collection. Rose's ensuing negotiations with the fair and the story of the New York *Aquacade* will be discussed in chapter 7.
25. Brooks Atkinson, *New York Times,* May 29, 1938.
26. Billy Rose, *New York Post,* July 20, 1938.
27. Anderson, p. 182.
28. Rose's penchant for the 1890s can be seen as early as 1924 with his investment in *The Fatal Wedding* (see chapter 1).
29. Zolotow, p. 523.
30. Scheff's fur was delivered each night in an armored car which returned it to the furrier immediately after her curtain call. "Kiss Me Again" was originally deleted from *Mlle. Modiste* because Scheff felt it unsuited to her range. On opening night in New York, Victor Herbert pleaded with her to sing it for him as a Christmas present. It soon became her best-loved song.
31. Anderson, p. 183.
32. Diamond Horseshoe table card, circa 1938, Billy Rose Theatre Collection.
33. Zolotow, p. 523.
34. Anderson, p. 68.
35. Zolotow, p. 523.
36. Ibid.
37. Program for *The Big Show,* 1939, Billy Rose Theatre Collection.
38. *New York News,* April 11, 1939.
39. Anderson, pp. 189-97. All other Diamond Horseshoe shows were collaborations between Rose and Anderson. *The Silver Screen*'s success in New York led Anderson to stage a Hollywood version at the Willshire Bowl in Los Angeles that lost more than $20,000 in three weeks.

152 Notes for Chapter 7

40. Typescript for *It's Fun to Be Free* by Billy Rose and Ben Hecht, 1943, Billy Rose Theatre Collection. A variation on this show was also presented at Madison Square Garden as a USO benefit.

41. Ibid. While the show made the usual wartime play on anti-Axis sentiment, not all of it was accomplished in good taste. Ben Hecht wrote the following introduction for Eddie Cantor that Rose and Cantor wisely removed from the show:

> When you call the roll of the nation's laugh makers for the past two generations, what do you find? Jews. Lots of Jews. Witty, clownish, capering, idiotic and humpty-dumpty Jews.... God knows what makes Jews comedians. But there they are—belaboring the land with their lusty and zany humors.... The Marx Brothers, Fanny Brice, Charlie Chaplin and Milton Berle.... At the head of this cavalcade stands New York's own gusty and unquenchable Eddie Cantor.

42. Anderson, pp. 187–88.

43. Anderson, p. 182.

44. John McCabe, *George M. Cohan: The Man Who Owned Broadway* (New York: Doubleday and Co., 1973), p. 67.

Chapter 7

1. Morton Eustis, "Big Show in Flushing Meadows," *Theatre Arts Monthly,* (August 1939), p. 567.

2. F. Scott Fitzgerald, *The Great Gatsby* (New York: Chas. Scribner's Sons, 1925, reprint ed., 1953), p. 23.

3. Stanley Appelbaum, introduction to *The New York World's Fair 1939/1940* (New York: Dover Publications, 1977), p. 9.

4. Zolotow, p. 424. The decision to open the fair on April 30, 1939 (the 150th anniversary of Washington's inaugural), was made when it became apparent that the exposition would be ready several months ahead of original projections. Aside from a large statue of Washington, however, the fair ultimately made little effort to tie the event in with its futuristic theme and overall design. The fair's director of research, Dr. Frank Monaghan, did arrange a reenactment of Washington's journey from Mount Vernon to New York, but the stunt generated little interest.

5. Anderson, p. 178. This was several years before the government-sponsored radio network of the same name.

6. Conrad, p. 121.

7. Ibid.

8. Conrad, p. 122. Twenty-five years later when Moses was in charge of the 1964 New York World's Fair, Rose urged him to include a viable midway with an attraction that would help the fair meet its ongoing costs. Moses felt that his fair did not require any flashy amusements to survive. Rose warned that without an *Aquacade*-style spectacle, Moses would "lose twenty-five million dollars of somebody's money." The 1964 fair actually lost more than thirty million dollars.

9. *Aquacade* production records, 1939, Billy Rose Theatre Collection.

10. Zolotow, p. 422.

Notes for Chapter 7

11. Ibid. Rose later blamed high prices for the fair's disappointing attendance. "New York cut its throat with a 75 cent general admission and over priced restaurants," he said. "When they heard in Decatur, Illinois that it cost $12 to dine at the New York World's Fair French Pavilion, Mama and Poppa decided to stay home and listen to Bing Crosby."
12. Anderson, p. 179.
13. Zolotow, p. 428.
14. Ibid., p. 430.
15. *Aquacade* correspondence and financial records, 1939, Billy Rose Theatre Collection.
16. Conrad, p. 126.
17. Zolotow, pp. 424–27.
18. Ibid. The governor granted Rose a trial period to determine if his ballyhoo for the *Aquacade* was out of character with the rest of the fair. Although Rose reduced the size of his sign in 1940, the *Aquacade* had long since become a standing-room-only attraction.
19. The amphitheatre's stage was 311 feet wide compared to the 128-foot stage used in Cleveland. Ten thousand people could be accommodated at the New York *Aquacade* as opposed to approximately seven thousand at Cleveland.
20. *Aquacade* program, 1939, Billy Rose Collection.
21. Ibid. The beach ball sequence was cut for the 1940 edition as it was almost impossible to perform on windy days.
22. Ibid.
23. Brooks Atkinson, *New York Times*, May 5, 1939.
24. Zolotow, p. 435.
25. Burns Mantle, *New York News*, May 5, 1939.
26. Brooks Atkinson, *New York Times*, May 5, 1939.
27. Papers of the Press and Promotion Department, New York World's Fair, 1939, Manuscript Division, Drawer 7, Box 2, New York Public Library, New York, New York. The show was normally presented four times a day.
28. Zolotow, p. 435. Rose's fair income was enhanced by his Barbary Coast saloon concession which featured many popular acts from the Diamond Horseshoe (see chapter 5). This nightclub-style entertainment also had a successful stint at San Francisco's Golden Gate Exposition in 1940.
29. *New York Herald Tribune*, March 26, 1939.
30. Lucius Beebe, *New York Herald Tribune*, n.d. From *Aquacade* scrapbook, Billy Rose Collection.
31. Souvenir program, New York World's Fair, 1939, p. 46.
32. *New York Post*, May 11, 1939. While there were a few raised eyebrows, most New Yorkers had seen far more lascivious entertainments in nightclubs and revues than ever graced the New York World's Fair. In fact, the juxtaposition of sophisticated pavilions and architecture with the exuberantly tawdry midway, made the fair a far more interesting and complex event.
33. Zolotow, p. 441.

34. *Aquacade* programs, Billy Rose Collection, Box 5, folder 11.
35. Zolotow, p. 451.
36. Ibid. Unlike his distress over the Shuberts' use of chubby showgirls *The Great Temptation* in 1925 (see chapter 1), Rose had some genuine cause to feel that Stein was attempting to steal his production. Although no concrete evidence exists to support the theory, it is not impossible that the Stein matter was simply a ploy by exposition officials to force Rose into producing the *Aquacade* in San Francisco.
37. *Aquacade* correspondence, 1940, Billy Rose Theatre Collection.
38. Jack James and Earle Weller, *Treasure Island, "The Magic City": The Story of the Golden Gate International Exposition* (San Francisco: Pisani Printing and Publishing Company, 1941), p. 25.
39. *Aquacade* financial records, 1940, Billy Rose Theatre Collection.
40. *San Francisco Chronicle,* May 13, 1940.
41. *San Francisco Chronicle,* May 27, 1940.
42. By comparison, only 26 percent of those who attended the New York World's Fair saw the New York *Aquacade.*
43. Based on attendance figures compiled by the Bureau of International Expositions and the New York World's Fair Research and Library Department. The *Aquacade*s even outdrew such famous attractions as Little Egypt and the Ferris Wheel at the Columbian Exposition and Sally Rand at the 1933 Chicago Fair. Rose contemplated a touring version of the show until studies showed that the technical problems were too formidable.
44. Brussels staged the first postwar world's fair in 1958.
45. Zolotow, p. 440. Rose's point is well taken, if inelegantly expressed. While world's fairs continue to rely on displays of modern technology and commerce, the traditional exposition foreign village concession has begun to lose favor with world's fair planners. Ironically, the village motif originally pioneered by the Columbian Exposition now finds its most vital contemporary expression in such outdoor amusement complexes as the theme parks and Disney environments, in which they provide appropriate architectural set dressing for the sale of various foreign foods and souvenirs.
46. Ibid. Rose still believed a permanent fair was possible and made various attempts to explore this notion over the next fifteen years (see chapter 8).
47. *New York Herald Tribune,* 1940, n.d., *Aquacade* scrapbook, Billy Rose Theatre Collection.

Chapter 8

1. Ernest Hemingway quoted by A. E. Hotchner in "Hemingway as Playwright," *Playbill,* 1967, p. 11.
2. Ibid.
3. Ibid.
4. Richard Watts, *New York,* March 1940.
5. Hotchner, p. 12.
6. Billy Rose to Benjamin Glazer, April 22, 1940, Billy Rose Theatre Collection.

7. Ibid. Rose's forecast proved completely accurate.
8. Harold Clurman, *The Fervent Years: The Group Theatre and the Thirties* (New York: Alfred A. Knopf, 1945; reprint ed., New York: Da Capo Press, 1983), p. 275. Odets's subsequent association with Rose probably spelled the end of the Group Theatre. Although Odets and Strasberg claimed that the Group was already defunct, Harold Clurman later maintained that Rose lured Strasberg and Odets away and hastened the Group's demise.
9. Zolotow, p. 493.
10. Ibid. Rose later referred to Bankhead as "Humphrey Bogart in lace panties."
11. Zolotow, p. 495.
12. Ibid., p. 496.
13. Production notes, *Clash by Night*, 1941, Billy Rose Theatre Collection.
14. Wolcott Gibbs, *The New Yorker*, January 5, 1942.
15. Brooks Atkinson, *New York Times*, December 29, 1941.
16. Burns Mantle, n.p., December 28, 1941.
17. John Mason Brown, *New York World Telegram*, January 25, 1942. Brown, who had earlier referred to the show as "Odets's Tobacco Road Othello," thanked Rose profusely in print for this gift.
18. Ben Hecht, introduction to souvenir program for Washington, D.C. performance of *We Will Never Die*, April 12, 1943, Billy Rose Theatre Collection.
19. Ben Hecht, *We Will Never Die* typescript, March 1943, Billy Rose Theatre Collection.
20. Ibid.
21. Ibid.
22. Ibid.
23. Many contributors were put off by Hecht's avid support of Jewish guerrilla groups in Palestine.
24. Wolcott Gibbs, *The New Yorker*, September 14, 1946.
25. Zolotow, p. 502.
26. Zolotow, p. 509.
27. Conrad, p. 158. Although Hearst obviously saw some newsworthiness in Rose's novel show, no pictures of the black cast appeared in either the *Journal* or the *Mirror*.
28. George Freedley, *New York Morning Telegraph*, December 4, 1943.
29. Robert Garland, *New York Journal-American*, December 3, 1943; Lewis Nichols, *New York Times*, December 3, 1943.
30. Zolotow, p. 512.
31. *Variety*, December 8, 1943.
32. Zolotow, p. 512.
33. Conrad, p. 160. Despite the objective evidence, there is still some question as to whether Rose staged the ticket mix-up as a publicity stunt. It was certainly not out of character, although the risks seem to argue against the incident's premeditation.

Notes for Chapter 8

34. *Carmen Jones* was a landmark for opera in other respects as well. Its emphasis on American talent and production values was to have a great influence on the growth of innovative regional opera companies such as the Houston Grand Opera and the Santa Fe Opera. Along with George Gershwin's *Porgy and Bess* and Scott Joplin's *Treemonisha, Carmen Jones* established the fact that American artists could make substantial aesthetic contributions to the opera.

35. Conrad, p. 162. Rose's maneuverings on this particular transaction were worthy of the late J. P. Morgan. Howard Barnes wrote that his "strategy would have confounded Richelieu." Rose later told a friend that consummating the deal was "as tough as playing the Gershwin rhapsody on a ten-cent harmonica" (Conrad, p. 166).

36. Lucius Beebe, *New York Herald Tribune*, November 1944.

37. John Lahr, *Notes on a Cowardly Lion* (New York: Alfred A. Knopf, 1970), p. 232. At the time, many people felt that a $1.5-million revue was in poor taste during the austerity of wartime. Rose's decision to premiere the production on the anniversary of Pearl Harbor hardly helped the situation. Just before the opening night curtain, Bert Lahr went to Bea Lillie's dressing room to wish her luck. He found the famous actress in tears. "I didn't say anything," Lahr recalled. "It was about then, I think, that her son was missing in action. And now, on Pearl Harbor Day, she was going on.... I knew how she felt" (Lahr, p. 233).

38. Charles Schwartz, *Cole Porter* (New York: Dial Press, 1977; reprint ed., New York: Da Capo Press, 1979), p. 217. Stravinsky's work was finally performed in its entirety in the winter of 1945 by the New York Philharmonic.

39. Lahr, p. 231. Lahr's refusal to do the song irked Porter, who years later remarked to Lahr's wife Mildred, "Your husband doesn't think I can write a comedy song" (ibid.).

40. Lahr, p. 230.

41. "Drink, Drink, Drink," music and lyrics by Cole Porter, 1944, Billy Rose Theatre Collection. The song was Lahr's best-received number in the show.

42. *Billboard*, December 2, 1944.

43. Ibid.

44. Advertisement for *Seven Lively Arts, New York Daily News*, November 21, 1944. The show's advance totaled more than $500,000, roughly four times the average Broadway presale in 1944.

45. Dali's subjects were entitled: "Movies," "Opera," "Ballet," "Jive," "Theatre," "Concert" and "Radio."

46. Lucius Beebe, *New York Herald Tribune*, December 8, 1944.

47. *Time*, December 18, 1944.

48. Lewis Nichols, *New York Times*, December 8, 1944.

49. *New York Herald Tribune*, December 8, 1944.

50. *Billboard*, December 2, 1944.

51. Robert Garland, *New York Journal-American*, December 8, 1944.

52. Zolotow, p. 519.

53. Ibid. *Seven Lively Arts* was indeed Rose's last Broadway musical. His ensuing stint as a columnist and the protracted public divorce battle with Holm quelled his desire for highly

publicized grandiose productions. He also knew that the economics of Broadway had changed and that shows such as *Seven Lively Arts* had become too great a risk for any single producer.

54. As was the case with his earlier career as a songwriter, the origin of Rose's journalistic talents was subject to widespread speculation. Although he did maintain a substantial staff of ghostwriters and researchers, most of the pieces bore the stamp of his chatty, jargon-laden style. Lee Rogow, one of Rose's principle ghosts, later noted that Rose either wrote or supervised every word. "There was never a word, comma or punctuation mark that escaped his notice.... Once we slaved for six hours over a single paragraph" (Gottlieb, p. 179). The column's popularity led to "The Billy Rose Show," an ill-fated ABC television series produced by Jed Harris.

55. Conrad, p. 190. Rose apparently had similar conversations with dozens of other editors. Correspondence and promotional materials in the Billy Rose Theatre Collection indicate that Rose viewed the column as little more than an ongoing national self-advertisement. One flyer ballyhooing the column began, "Move over, de Maupassant!"

56. Gottlieb, p. 193.

57. Ruth and Augustus Goetz, "Adapting Gide's *The Immoralist*," New York Times, January 31, 1954.

58. Ibid.

59. Billy Rose, *New York Herald Tribune*, January 31, 1954.

60. Goetz.

61. *Variety*, February 10, 1954.

62. Brooks Atkinson, *New York Times*, February 9, 1954.

63. Gottlieb, p. 221.

64. *New York Times*, December 15, 1955.

65. *New York Times*, June 6, 1955.

66. Conrad, p. 260.

67. Rose, p. 28.

68. To be sure, many of Rose's production values are in evidence today. The lavish floor shows of the major Las Vegas and Atlantic City nightclubs, the various live entertainments offered in the nation's theme parks, and the recent resurgence of cabaret-style revues and nightclub performance are all closely related to Rose's style of theatre. A more direct example of Rose's influence was seen at the 1984 New Orleans World's Fair, which presented an *Aquacade* patterned on Rose's model, some forty-five years after the Holm-Weissmuller spectacular in New York. David Wolper's 1986 Liberty Weekend extravaganza in New York City is yet another instance of the Rosean approach to spectacle.

69. Goetz.

70. *Time*, December 18, 1944.

71. Conrad, p. 271.

72. Ben Hecht, *Child of the Century* (New York: Simon and Schuster, 1954), p. 225.

73. Ibid.

Bibliography

A Note on the Sources

Most of the primary material consulted in the preparation of this study can be found at the New York Public Library. The Billy Rose Theatre Collection of the New York Public Library at Lincoln Center contains extensive correspondence, production notes, prompt scripts, photographs, clippings, programs and other pertinent material from all of Rose's productions, including his exposition entertainments at Fort Worth and Cleveland. These materials provide a thorough and detailed record of Rose's entire theatrical career. In addition, the collection contains rare newsreel footage from the New York *Aquacade* and *Jumbo*. The National Archives in Washington also have an excellent newsreel collection which contains several minutes of footage from the New York *Aquacade*. The records of the 1939 New York World's Fair (housed in the New York Public Library's Manuscript Division) provide a fascinating picture of Rose's most famous production and his often stormy relationship with fair officials. Supporting documentation from the California and Chicago historical societies was of great value in preparing the chapters on Rose's other world's fair productions. Interviews with people who saw various Billy Rose shows helped provide a clearer picture of the audience impact of these productions.

Collections

Chicago, Illinois. Chicago Historical Society. Collection of materials on Century of Progress Exposition of 1933.
———. University of Illinois. Official records of the Century of Progress Exposition of 1933.
New York, New York. Actors' Equity Theatre Collection. Robert F. Wagner Labor Archives. Contracts and correspondence pertaining to various Billy Rose enterprises.
———. Museum of the City of New York. Theatre and Music Collection. Drawings and photographs, Diamond Horseshoe nightclub, 1943-1946.
———. New York Public Library. Billy Rose Theatre Collection. Billy Rose Collection. Papers and ephemera of the late Billy Rose, 1925-1965.
———. New York Public Library. Billy Rose Theatre Collection. Billy Rose Collection. Maurice Zolotow, *Billy Rose of Broadway*. Unpublished manuscript, 1945.
———. New York Public Library. Manuscript Division. Official papers and ephemera, 1939 New York World's Fair.
———. The Shubert Archive. Production material and clippings, *Carmen Jones,* 1943.
San Francisco, California. California Historical Society. Programs, photographs and ephemera, 1939 Golden Gate Exposition.
Washington, D.C. National Archives. Newsreel footage of 1939 New York *Aquacade*.

Interviews

Boch, Robert. Columbus, Ohio. October 26, 1984.
Sedutto, Martha. New York, New York. January 12, 1985.
Wilson, Mrs. E. L. San Francisco, California. November 20, 1984.

Books and Manuscripts

Abbott, George. *Mister Abbott.* New York: Random House, 1963.
Allwood, John. *The Great Expositions.* London: Studio Vista, 1977.
Anderson, John Murray. *Out without My Rubbers.* New York: Library Publishers, 1953.
Appelbaum, Stanley. *The New York World's Fair 1939/1940.* New York: Dover Publications, 1977.
Aronson, Arnold. *The History and Theory of Environmental Scenography.* Ann Arbor, Michigan: UMI Research Press, 1977.
Atkinson, Brooks. *Broadway Scrapbook.* New York: Theatre Arts, 1947.
Badger, Reid. *The Great American Fair.* Chicago: Nelson-Hall, 1979.
Benedict, Burton, ed. *The Anthropology of World's Fairs.* Berkeley: Scolar Press, 1983.
Blackburn, Sara, ed. *Dawn of a New Day: The New York World's Fair, 1939/40.* New York: New York University Press, 1980.
Blesh, Rudi and Harriet Janis. *They All Played Ragtime.* New York: Oak Publications, 1966.
Bloom, Sol. *The Autobiography of Sol Bloom.* New York: G. P. Putnam's Sons, 1948.
Boles, Don. *The Midway Showman.* Atlanta: Pinchpenny Press, 1967.
Braithwaite, David. *Fairground Architecture: The World of Amusement Parks, Carnivals, and Fairs.* New York: F. A. Praeger, 1968.
Brockett, Oscar. *History of the Theatre.* Boston: Allyn and Bacon, 1977.
Carlson, Raymond, ed. *National Directory of Theme Parks and Amusement Areas.* New York: Pilot Books, 1978.
Clarke, Norman. *The Mighty Hippodrome.* New York: Barnes, 1968.
Clurman, Harold. *The Fervent Years: The Group Theatre and the Thirties.* New York: Alfred A. Knopf, 1945; reprint ed., New York: Da Capo Press, 1983.
Conrad, Earl. *Manhattan Primitive.* New York: World Publishing, 1968.
"Environmental Entertainment (Amusement Parks and Theme Parks)." In *American Popular Entertainment,* edited by Myron Matlaw. London: Greenwood Press, 1979.
Epstein, Milton. "The New York Hippodrome: From Luna Park to Sixth Avenue." M.A. thesis, New York University, 1980.
Fitzgerald, F. Scott. *The Great Gatsby.* New York: Chas. Scribner's Sons, 1925. Reprinted, 1953.
Gilbert, Douglas. *American Vaudeville, Its Life and Times.* New York: Dover, 1953.
Gottlieb, Polly Rose. *The Nine Lives of Billy Rose.* New York: Crown Publishers, 1968.
Gressler, Thomas Henry. "John Murray Anderson: Director of Reviews." Ph.D. dissertation, Kent State University, 1973.
Hart, Moss. *Act One.* New York: Random House, 1959.
Hecht, Ben. *Child of the Century.* New York: Simon and Schuster, 1954.
Hilton, Suzanne. *Here Today and Gone Tomorrow: The Story of World's Fairs and Expositions.* Philadelphia: Westminster Press, 1978.
James, Jack and Earle Weller. *Treasure Island, "The Magic City": The Story of the Golden Gate International Exposition.* San Francisco: Printing and Publishing Company, 1941.
Katkov, Norman. *The Fabulous Fanny.* New York: Alfred A. Knopf, 1953.
Lahr, John. *Notes on a Cowardly Lion.* New York: Alfred A. Knopf, 1970.
Maney, Richard. *Fanfare: The Confessions of a Press Agent.* New York: Harper & Brothers, 1957.

McCabe, John. *George M. Cohan: The Man Who Owned Broadway.* New York: Doubleday and Co., 1973.

McCullough, Edo. *World's Fair Midway: An Affectionate Account of American Amusement Areas from the Crystal Palace to the Crystal Ball.* New York: Arno Press, 1966.

McKechnie, Samuel. *Popular Entertainments through the Ages.* 1931. Reprinted, New York: Benjamin Blom, 1969.

Morehouse, Ward. *Forty-Five Minutes from Broadway.* New York: Dial Press, 1939.

Nathan, George Jean. *The Entertainment of a Nation.* New York: Alfred A. Knopf, 1942.

_____. *The Popular Theatre.* New York: Alfred A. Knopf, 1918.

Parks, Melvin. *Musicals of the 1930s.* New York: Museum of the City of New York, 1966.

Rose, Billy. *Wine, Women and Words.* New York: Simon and Schuster, 1946.

Schwartz, Charles. *Cole Porter.* New York: Dial Press, 1977.

Seldes, Gilbert. *The Seven Lively Arts.* 1924. Reprinted, Cranbury, New Jersey: A. S. Barnes, 1962.

Smith, Cecil. *Musical Comedy in America.* New York: Theatre Arts Books, 1950.

Taylor, Deems. *Some Enchanted Evenings: The Story of Rodgers and Hammerstein.* New York: Harper, 1953.

Turnbusch, Tom. *Complete Production Guide to Modern Musical Theatre.* New York: Richards Rosen Press, 1969.

Wilder Alex. *American Popular Song: The Great Innovators, 1900–1950.* New York: Oxford University Press, 1971.

Wilmeth, Don B. *Variety Entertainment and Outdoor Amusements.* Westport, Connecticut: Greenwood Press, 1983

Winter, William. *The Life of David Belasco.* 2 vols. New York: Irvington, 1920.

Articles

Cochran, Charles B. "The Revue as an Art Form." *Forthnightly Review*, September 1925, pp. 359–62.

cummings, e.e. "Coney Island." *Vanity Fair*, June 1926.

The Drama Review, March 1974, special issue on popular entertainment.

Eustis, Morton. "Big Show in Flushing Meadows." *Theatre Arts Monthly*, August 1939, p. 567.

Gibbs, Wolcott. "A Little Something for Almost Everybody." *The New Yorker*, December 19, 1953, p. 75.

Goetz, Ruth and Augustus. "Adapting Gide's *The Immoralist*." *New York Times*, January 31, 1954.

Leighton, George R. "World's Fairs: From Little Egypt to Robert Moses." *Harper's Magazine*, July 1960, pp. 27–37.

McNamara, Brooks. "Popular Scenography." *The Drama Review*, March 1974, pp. 16–24.

Reed, Edward. "American Theatre Designers." *The American Magazine of Art*, May 1940, p. 277.

Seldes, Gilbert. "Stage-Door Johnny, Pro-Tem." *Esquire*, September 1934, p. 137.

"Theme Parks." *Theatre Crafts*, September 1977, entire issue.

Periodicals and Newspapers

In addition to the previously listed sources, the following publications were referred to extensively for reviews and commentary on individual productions:

The American Dancer, 1937–1940.
Billboard, 1924–1954.

Brooklyn Daily Eagle, 1929–1936.
Cleveland Plain Dealer, 1937.
Fort Worth Star-Telegram, 1936.
New York Daily News, 1925–1954.
New York Herald Tribune, 1929–1944.
New York Mirror, 1930–1944.
New York Post, 1935–1954.
New York Sun, 1930–1944.
New York Times, 1925–1966.
New York World Telegram, 1930–1944.
The New Yorker, 1935–1954.
San Francisco Chronicle, 1940.
Theatre Arts Monthly, 1935–1940.
Vanity Fair, 1930–1935.
Variety, 1924–1944.

Index

Abbott, Bud, 87
Abbott, George, 21, 31, 35
Abie's Irish Rose (Nichols), 9
Actors' Equity, 36
Adler, Luther, 124
Ager, Cecilia, 128
Aircade project, 139
Albee, Edward, 139
Alcohol Control Board, 39
Allan Foster Girls, 42
Allen, Fred, 88
Alter, Lou, 16
Alton, Robert, 61, 91; choreography for *Aquacade* of Cleveland, 73-74; choreography for *Aquacade* of New York, 104; choreography for Fort Worth Frontier Centennial, 52, 54, 57
Alvord, Ned, 19-20, 30, 36, 70; promoting *Crazy Quilt*, 21; promoting Fort Worth Frontier Centennial, 52, 53, 54
American Guild of Variety Artists, 36
Anderson, John Murray, x, 20-21, 81, 88, 90, 94, 98, 99; staging the *Aquacade* of Cleveland, 70, 73; staging the *Aquacade* of New York, 102, 104; staging the *Aquacade* of San Francisco, 115; staging at the Diamond Horseshoe, 89; staging the Fort Worth Frontier Centennial, 52, 53, 54, 55, 58, 61; staging The Great Lakes Exposition, 65, 68; staging *Jumbo*, 31, 32, 33, 34, 35, 38, 40, 42; staging *The Silver Screen*, 91-93
Andrews, Earl, 80
"Any Bonds Today," 93
"Anything Goes" (Porter), 59
Aquacade of Cleveland (produced by Rose), 65-66, 68-76, 79; "A Beach in California," 71; "Coney Island, 1905," 74; designs for, 70; "Half and Half" number, 73-74, fig. 18; "It Can't Happen Here" number, 74; reviews of, 76; sources of, 76

Aquacade of New York (produced by Rose), 91, 99-100, 103-7, 135; changes for 1940, 113; reviews of, 107-8, 112; swim audition, 101
Aquacade of San Francisco (produced by Rose), 114, 115, 118
"Arctic Girl's Tomb of Ice," 108
Arlen, Harold, 21
Armstrong, Harry, 90
Arno, Peter, 14, 15
Arnstein, Nicky, 11
Aronson, Boris, 123
Arronsen, Max, 9, 22
Artists and Models (produced by Shuberts), 16, 129
Atkinson, Brooks: reviews *Aquacade* of New York, 104, 107; reviews *Clash by Night*, 123; reviews *The Great Magoo*, 21; reviews *The Immoralist*, 138; reviews *Jumbo*, 42; reviews *Streamlined Varieties*, 87

Backstage Club, 8-10, 11
Baker, Phil, 17
Bankhead, Tallulah, 40, 122, 124, 132; on Rose, 123
"Barney Google" (Rose), 7, 8
Barnum, P.T., ix, 19, 30, 45, 66
Barr, David, 139
Barton, James, 16, 17, 91
Baruch, Bernard, 2, 3, 29, 30, 32, 33, 77, 119
Basie, Count (William Basie), 128
Bates, Lulu, 57, 89, 90
Bay, Howard, 128
Beck, Helen Gould. *See* Rand, Sally
Beebe, Lucius, 19, 23, 107, 132, 135
Beekman Place, 2, 118, 119, 122
Belasco, David, 45, 65
Bel Geddes, Norman, 132
Ben Ami, Jacob, 124, 126
Ben Hecht, S.S., 126

Benny, Jack, 87, 93, 94
Berkeley, Busby, 14, 66, 73
Berle, Milton, 94
Berlin, Irving, 8, 40
The Big Show (produced by Rose), 91, 132
Billboard, 44, 134, 135
"A Bird in a Gilded Cage," 90
Bizet, Georges, 127, 129
Borach, Fannie. *See* Brice, Fanny
Brando, Marlon, 124, 126
Brice, Fanny, 8, 13, 25, 28, 29, 40, 46, 47, 58; breakup with Rose, 77, 79, 136; in *Corned Beef and Roses*, 14, 15, 16; meets Rose, 11; parties, 11, 30; in *Sweet and Low,* 17
Broadway Theatre, 129
Brooklyn Dodgers, 93
Bruckner, Richard, 53
Brundage, Avery, 67
Burke, Billie, 135
Burr, Eugene, 44
Butterfield 8 (Mann), 137
"By the Beautiful Sea," 74

Cahoon, Wyn, 56
Cantor, Eddie, 93
Carmen (Bizet), 127, 129
Carmen Jones (Hammerstein), 128–31, 132, 156n.34; compared to *Carmen,* 127
Carousel. See The Great Magoo
Carpenter, Constance, 11
Carroll, Earl, 14
Carter, Amon, 47–48, 50, 52, 60
Casa Mañana (Fort Worth), 53, 58, 62, 63, 64, 65, 66, 69, 70, 76, 77, 113; film about, 81; "It Can't Happen Here" number, 74; 1937 edition, 60–61; noble gigolos at, 60; reviews of, 60; revue at, 59, 60
Casa Mañana (New York), 81, 83, 88, 132; closing, 91; Palm Beach Bar at, 81, fig. 20; *Streamlined Varieties* at, 87, 91
Casino de Paree, 23–25, 29, 30, 32, 53, 60, 71, 76, 79, 81
Century of Progress Exposition (Chicago), 51, 63, 84
Chapman, John, 129
Chase, Chaz, 23
"Cheerful Little Earful" (Gershwin, Warren, and Rose), 7, 14
"The Circus Is on Parade" (Rogers and Hart), 41
Cirque d'Hiver, 30
Cirque Medrano, 30
Clash by Night (Odets), 122, 123, 124, 132
Cleveland Exposition. *See* The Great Lakes Exposition

Clurman, Harold, 122
Cobb, Lee J., 120, 123
Cochran, Charles B., 13
Cody, Buffalo Bill, 45
Cohan, George M., 95, 107
Cole, Jack, 91
Coll, Vincent "Mad Dog," 9
Columbian Exposition (1893), 50, 56
Compton, Betty, 11
Coney Island's Luna Park, ix, 32
Conn, Chester, 7
Conrad, Earl, x, 19
Corned Beef and Roses (produced by Rose), 14–16, 134; "Angel Ballet" number, 16; "Poor Mr. Shufeld" number, 15; "Stocks and Blondes" number, 16
Cornell, Katherine, 25
Costello, Lou, 87
Cotton, Faye, 53, 59
Crabbe, Buster, 113
Crawford, Joan, 39
Crazy Quilt (produced by Rose), 17, 19, 20, 21, 22, 76, 79, 132
Crockett, Davy, 50
Crystal Palace (London), 51
Cummings, Homer, 29

"Dainty Quainty Me" (Porter), 133
Daley, Richard, 83
Dali, Salvador, 112, 135
Daly, Augustin, 65
Dare, Danny, 14
Davis, Gussie, 8
Dean, James, 137
Delmonico's, 89
De Mille, Cecil B., 30, 99
DeMotte, Josie, 42
Dempsey, Jack, 40
Dewey, Thomas, 124
Diamond Horseshoe, 88–91, 94, 112, 118, 123, 136; *It's Fun to Be Free* at, 93; *Mrs. Astor's Pet Horse* at, 91; *The Silver Screen* at, 91, 93; *The Turn of the Century* at, 90; *Violins over Broadway* at, 94
Dickey, Lincoln, 64–65, 74, 100, 101, 113–14
Disney, Walt, 88, 93
Dixon, Mort, 6–7, 8, 14
"Does the Spearmint lose its flavor on the bedpost overnight?," 7
Dolin, Anton, 132, 135
Dowell, Mary, 61, 83, 93
Downey, Morton, 83, 103
"Dream of Venus" (Dali), 112
Dubin, Al, 6–7, 8

duBois, Raoul Pène, 91, 98; costumes for *Aquacade* of Cleveland, 68; costumes for *Aquacade* of New York, 101; costumes for *Carmen Jones,* 128; costumes for Fort Worth Frontier Centennial, 52, 58, 59; costumes for *Jumbo,* 31, 35; costumes for *Let's Play Fair,* 83–84, 86
Dundy, Elmer, ix, 30, 33, 65
Dunnigan, John, 80
Durante, Jimmy, 56; in *Jumbo,* 36, 39, 41, 42
Durocher, Leo, 93

Eddy, Eddie, 23, 57, 90
Ederle, Gertrude, 104
Elsa Maxwell Girls, 83
Eternal Road, 33
Eustis, Morton, 97
"Ev'ry Time We Say Goodbye," 133

Fairs, 63, 98, 118, 154n.45
The Fatal Wedding (Davis), 8
Ferrer, José, 140
Fifth Avenue Club, 10, 11
The Fifth Column (Hemingway), 119, 120–21
Fisher, Fred, 81, 91
Fitzgerald, F. Scott, 97
Floradora, 51
Forrest Theatre, 134
Fort Worth Athletic Club, 49
Fort Worth Frontier Centennial, 49, 50, 60, 67; Nude Ranch at, 58; opening of, 58–60; preparations for, 52–58
Fort Worth Frontier Fiesta, 60
46th Street Theatre, 16
Foster, Allan, 31–32, 42
Fowler, Gene, 21
Foy, Eddie, 56
Frazee Sisters, 74, 86
Freedley, George, 129
Freedman, David, 14, 16
French Casino, 77, 81
Friedman, Charles, 128
Fulton Theatre, 22

Gable, Clark, 53
Gabriel, Gilbert, 42
Gallo Theatre, 22
Garbo, Greta, 93, 112
Gardner, Ava, 51
Garland, Robert: reviews *Carmen Jones,* 129; reviews *The Great Magoo,* 21; reviews *Seven Lively Arts,* 135
Gershwin, Ira, 7, 14, 15
Geva, Tamara, 16
Gibbs, Wolcott, 13, 123, 126
Gibson, Harvey, 112–13

Gide, André, 137, 138
Gish, Lillian, 140
"Give Them Girls," 86
Glazer, Benjamin, 120, 121
Goetz, Augustus and Ruth, 137, 138
Golden Gate Exposition, 1939, 113, 114, 118
Gomez and Winoma, 59
Gone with the Wind (Mitchell), 61
Goodman, Benny: at Casino de Paree, 23, 29; in *Seven Lively Arts,* 132, 135
"Good Old Summer Time," 58, 74
Gordon, Max, 127
Gottlieb, Polly Rose (sister of Billy Rose), x
Gould, Barney, 113
Grafton, Gloria, 56; in *Jumbo,* 36, 41, 42
Gray, Beatrice, 132
Gray, Gilda, 89, 93
The Great Gatsby (Fitzgerald), 97
The Great Lakes Exposition, 63, 64, 77, 98; *Parade of the Years* at, 64
The Great Magoo (Hecht and Fowler; produced by Rose), 21–22, 45, 119
The Great Temptation (produced by the Shuberts), 10
The Great Ziegfeld (Leonard), 47
Gregg, John, 2, 4
Gregg Shorthand Club, 2
Group Theatre, 122, 155n.8
Guinan, Texas, 91

Hammerstein, Oscar, 127, 128–29, 131
Hammerstein Theatre, 25
Hammond, John, 128
Hammond, Percy, 42
Hanneford, Poodles, 36
Harburg, E.Y., 21
Harris, Edna, 4, 5
Harris, Jed, 13–14, 21, 120
Hart, Lorenz, 10; music for *Jumbo,* 31, 34, 35, 41
Hart, Moss, 122, 124, 132, 133
"Have a Little Dream on Me" (Rose), 25
Hayes, Helen, 40, 67
Healy, Ted, 17
Hearst, William Randolph, Jr., 129, 131
Hecht, Ben, 21, 24, 67, 122, 132; on Rose, 140–41; script for *Jumbo,* 31, 34, 35, 39, 44–45; *We Will Never Die* project, 124, 126
The Heiress (James), 137
Hemingway, Ernest, 119, 120, 121
Hepburn, Katharine, 40
Herbert, Victor, 7, 90
Hippo Cirque, 55
Hippodrome, 33–34, 65, 88
Hoctor, Harriet, 61, 89

Holiday, Billie, 128
Holm, Eleanor, 66–68, 77, 79, 100, 104, 118, 119, 135; in *Aquacade* of Cleveland, 71, 74; in *Aquacade* of New York, 101, 103, 107, 115; breakup with Rose, 136
Holtz, Lou, 87, 91
Hoover, J. Edgar, 29
Horne, Lena, 129
Hotchner, A.E., 120
Hotel Paramount, 87
The Hot Mikado (produced by Todd), 109
Houston, Sam, 50
Howard, Joe, 90
Hutton, Betty, 87
Hylan, John, 80

"I Found a Million Dollar Baby in a Five and Ten Cent Store" (Rose), 7, 17
"If You Believe in Me" (Arlen, Rose, Harburg), 21
"I Knew Him before He Was Spanish," 16
The Immoralist (Gide), 137
The Immoralist (Goetzes), 137–38
Indian Summer (Herbert), 7
International Hall, 115
International Ladies Garment Workers' Union, 128
"In the Middle of the Night" (Rose), 11
Irwin, Lou, 67
It Can't Happen Here, 61
"It Happened in Chicago" (Rose), 59
"It Happened in Miami," 103
It's Fun to Be Free (produced by Rose), 93, 94
"I Wonder Who's Keeping Him Now" (Rose and Alter), 16
"I Wonder Who's Kissing Her Now" (Howard), 90

James, Henry, 137
Jarrett, Arthur, 66, 68
Jessel, George, 14, 15, 16, 17, 93, 112
Johnson, Albert, 91, 94; *Aquacade* designs, 70, 101; designs for Diamond Horseshoe, 88, 89; designs for Fort Worth, 52, 53, 55, 56, 61, 63; designs for The Great Lakes Exposition, 65, 68; designs for *Jumbo,* 31, 33, 34
Johnson, Van, 87
Jolson, Al, 8
Jourdan, Louis, 137
Jumbo (produced by Rose), 31–42, 48, 49, 52, 55, 56, 65, 66, 76, 79, 100, 118; "The Circus Wedding" finale, 42, 54; "Diavolo" episode, 36, 53; film rights, 45, 47; finances of, 45; plagiarism in, 44; radio serialization, 39

Kahn, Otto, 14
Kaufman, George S., 47, 124, 132
Kaufman, Wolfe, 129, 131
Kay, Beatrice, 90
Kaye, Danny, 87
Keith's Vaudeville, 4
Kennedy, Andy, 23
Kiralfy, Imre, ix, 45
Kirkpatrick, Mary, 8
"Kiss Me Again," 90
Krimsky, John, 77, 79–80, 108, 112, 113
Krueger, Stubby, 74, 103–4

LaGuardia, Fiorello, 98
Lahr, Bert, 132, 133, 135
Lardner, Ring, 14
Lasky, Jesse, 22–23
The Last Frontier (produced by Rose), 53–55
Lawrence, Bob, 71
Lee, James, 87–88
Leftwich, Alexander, 14
Lehman, Herbert H., 101, 102, 103
Le Maire, Rufus, 47–48, 50
Leonard, Eddie, 89, 90
Let's Play Fair (produced by Rose), 81–87, 98
Life Begins at 8:40 (produced by Shubert), 20
Liliom (Molnar), 120
Lillie, Beatrice, 132, 133–34, 135, 136
Lindy's, 5, 6, 8, 123
Little Egypt, 50
"Little Girl Blue," 41
Loeb, Philip, 132
Logan, Ella, 94
Lost Horizon (Hilton), 61
Lumet, Sidney, 126

MacArthur, Charles, 67; script for *Jumbo,* 31, 39, 44–45
McCrary, Tex, 139
MacKaye, Percy, 65
MacKaye, Steele, 65
McKinley, William, 1
Mademoiselle Modiste (Herbert), 90
Madison Square Garden, 32, 101, 124
Mamba's Daughters, 87
Maney, Richard, 19, 21, 30, 31, 36, 58, 60, 62, 70, 122; on Brice, 46; on Holm, 67; publicity for *Jumbo,* 35, 38, 40, 41
Manhattan, S. S., 67
Manhattan Opera House, 31
Manhattan Primitive (Conrad), x
Mann, Daniel, 137
Mantle, Burns, 107, 123
Marden, Ben, 131
Markova, Alicia, 132, 135
Marquis, Don, 14

Marshall, Armina, 121
Marshall, Everett, 58, 61
Marx Brothers, 40
Matthews, Joyce, 136
Maxwell, Elsa, 48
"Meet Me in St. Louis, Louis," 58
Melba Sisters, 57
Mérimée, Prosper, 127
Merman, Ethel, 93
Metropolitan Opera, 88, 129, 135
MGM, 45, 47, 68, 81
Mielziner, Jo, 14–15
Minevitch, Borrah, and His Musical Rascals, 16
Miranda, Carmen, 93
Mitchell, Margaret, 61
Molnar, Ferenc, 120
Morehouse, Ward, 100
Morgan, Helen, 9, 87
Moses, Robert, 97, 113, 138–39; and Rose, 99, 100–101, 102–3, 152n.8
"The Most Beautiful Girl in the World," 41
Mrs. Astor's Pet Horse (produced by Rose), 91
Muni, Paul, 124, 126
Murray, Mae, 89, 93
Musical comedy, 45, 52
"My Romance," 41

Nathan, George Jean, 25
National Theatre, 139
New York American, 42
New Yorker, 123
New York Herald Tribune, 24, 36, 42, 86, 135
New York Journal-American, 129, 135
New York Mirror, 129
New York News, 91
"New York on Parade," 86
New York Post, 67, 87, 108–9
New York State Amphitheatre, 99, 101, 102
New York Times, 16, 129, 135
New York World, 17
New York World's Fair, 1939, 77, 79–80, 91, 95, 97, 98, 109; *Aquacade* project, 100–103; Barbary Coast project, 100, 101; prurient amusements at, 108–9
New York World Telegram, 21
Niblo's Garden, 65
Nichols, Anne, 9
Nichols, Lewis, 129, 135
Niesen, Gertrude, 23
"The Night Is Young and You're So Beautiful" (Suesse and Rose), 58
The Nine Lives of Billy Rose (Gottlieb), x
1919 National Shorthand Competition, 4
Novis, Donald, 36, 41, 42

Odets, Clifford, 122, 123, 140
Oklahoma! (Rogers and Hammerstein), 127
Olympics, 1936, 66
Ornstein, Charles, 87–88
Osborne, Paul, 136
Othello (Shakespeare), 122
Out without My Rubbers (Anderson), x
"Over and Over Again," 41

Page, Geraldine, 137
Patricola, Tom, 83, 89
Payson, Joan, 30
Pegler, Westbrook, 67, 108–9
Pennington, Ann, 58, 60, 89
Pins and Needles, 128
Pioneer Palace, 88, 100; at Fort Worth Frontier Centennial, 57; at The Great Lakes Exposition, 65, 69, 74
"Pitching Horseshoes" column, 136
Pitman shorthand, 2, 3
Polly of the Circus, 44
Porter, Cole, 59, 132, 133
Powell, Eleanor, 23, 29

Raft, George, 5
Rand, Sally, 51, 58, 59, 60, 83, 84, 112
Rapaport, Harry, 4
Rector's, 89
Reinhardt, Max, 33
Revue, 13
Riggin, Aileen, 65, 68
Ringling Brothers, 30
Ritz Theatre, 8
Robins, A., 42
Robinson, Bill "Bojangles," 93, 109, 129
Robinson, Edward G., 124
Rockefeller, John D., 10
Rockwell, Doc, 83, 84, 86, 132
Rodgers, Richard, 10, 31, 34, 35, 41
Rogers, Will, 48
"Roller Skating on a Rainbow" (Suesse and Rose), 103
Rose, Billy: and Bankhead, 122–23; on Billy Rose, 139; Billy Rose Music Hall, 25, 29, 32, 53, 81; Billy Rose Theatre, 139; Billy Rose Theatre Collection, x; character of, ix, 1, 21, 45, 77, 95, 113, 119, 127, 140; education of, ix, 2, 6, 14, 22; and Eleanor Holm, 68, 77, 79, 136; formula for entertainment, 8, 45, 52, 85–86, 90–91, 100; The Great Lakes Exposition work, 64–66, 68–76; legacy of, ix, x, 140, 157n.68; Matthews affair, 136; meets Moses, 99, 100–101, 102–3; and the mob, 9–10, 29, 146n.3; "Mr. Fanny Brice," 12,

Index

fig. 1, 31, 46, 47, 79; New York World's Fair projects, 98–99; opens Diamond Horseshoe, 88–90; operates the Backstage Club, 8–10; operates the Billy Rose Music Hall, 25, 29; operates the Casino de Paree, 22–25, 29; operates the Fifth Avenue Club, 10–11; opinions of, 62, 87, 88–89, 118, 140; "Pitching Horseshoes" column, 136; as pool hustler, 5–6; as promoter, 7, 19, 30, 81, 83–85, 86–87, 107; as stenographer, 2–4; unrealized projects, 139, 148n.12; "Why I'm Not a Legit Producer," 121–22; *Wine, Women and Words*, 136. Productions and songs: *Aquacade* of Cleveland, 66, 68–76; *Aquacade* of New York, 100–107; *Aquacade* of San Francisco, 114–18; "Barney Google," 7, 8; *The Big Show*, 91; *Billy Rose's Sins of 1926*, 10, 11; *Carmen Jones*, 128–31; "Cheerful Little Earful," 7, 14; *Clash by Night*, 121–24; *Corned Beef and Roses*, 14–16; *Crazy Quilt*, 17; "Does the Spearmint lose its flavor on the bedpost overnight?," 7; *The Fatal Wedding*, 8; *The Fifth Column*, 119–21; Fort Worth Frontier Centennial, 49–60; *The Great Magoo*, 21–22; "Have a Little Dream on Me," 25; "I Found a Million Dollar Baby in a Five and Ten Cent Store," 7, 17; "If You Believe in Me," 21; *The Immoralist*, 137–38; "In the Middle of the Night," 11; "I Wonder Who's Keeping Him Now," 16; *Jumbo*, 31–40; *Let's Play Fair*, 81–87; *Mrs. Astor's Pet Horse*, 91; "The Night Is Young and You're So Beautiful," 58; "Roller Skating on a Rainbow," 103; *Seven Lively Arts*, 132–36; *Show of Shows*, 79; "Small Time Cavalcade," 24, 30, 42, 57; *Streamlined Varieties*, 87; *Sweet and Low*, 16–17; "Throw a Little Party," 84; *The Turn of the Century*, 90; "Uncle Tom's Cabin Is a Roadhouse Now," 25; *Violins over Broadway*, 94; *We Will Never Die*, 124–26; *Who's Afraid of Virginia Woolf?*, 139; "Would You Like to Take a Walk," 14; "You're in Paree," 59. See also individual productions and songs
Rosenberg, David (father of Billy Rose), 1, 2, 3
Rosenberg, Fanny (mother of Billy Rose), 1–2, 3
Rosenberg, William Samuel. *See* Rose, Billy
Rosse, Herman, 20, 21, 94
Rossi, Angelo J., 114
Rothstein, Arnold, 9
Ruby, Harry, 6

Runyon, Damon, 60
Ruth, Babe, 36

Sadler's Wells, 65
St. Louis World's Fair of 1904, 58
San Francisco (Van Dyke II), 62
San Francisco Chronicle, 115, 118
Scandals (White), 57
Scheff, Fritzi, 89, 90, 151n.30
Schildkraut, Joseph, 123
Seldes, Gilbert, 131–32
Selwyn Theatre, 21
The Seven Lively Arts (produced by Rose), 132–36
Shagden, Joseph, 98
Shaw, Oscar, 81, 83, 84, 86
Short, Hassard, ix, 128, 132
Show of Shows, 79, 91
Shubert, J.J., 10, 80, 129
Shubert, Lee, 10, 131
Shultz, Dutch, 9
Shumlin, Herman, 137
The Silver Screen (produced by Anderson), 91, 93
Sissle, Noble, 93
Skelly, Hal, 14, 15, 16
"Small Time Cavalcade" (Rose and Hecht), 24, 30, 42, 57
Smith, Alison, 17
Smith, Muriel, 128
Stage, 121
Stein, Jules, 113, 114
"Strangers in the Dark," 74
Strasberg, Lee, 120, 122, 123
Stravinsky, Igor, 132, 133
Streamlined Varieties (produced by Rose), 87, 91
Streets of Paris (produced by the Shuberts), 109
"Striptease Susie," 57
Suesse, Dana, 103; music for *Aquacade* of Cleveland, 70; music for Fort Worth Frontier Centennial, 52, 58; music for *Let's Play Fair*, 81
"Sweet Adeline" (Armstrong), 90
Sweet and Low (produced by Rose), 16–17, 21, 76, 91, 132
Swope, Herbert Bayard, 30

"Take Me Out to the Ballgame," 94
Tammany Hall, 77, 131
Taylor, Deems, 129
Taylor, Elizabeth, 137
Television, 94, 118
Texaco, 39
"That Old Gang of Mine" (Dixon), 7

Theatre Arts Monthly, 97
Theatre Guild, 119, 120, 121
Thompson, Frederic, ix, 30, 33, 65
Thornton, Robert, 50
Three Stooges, 87
"Throw a Little Party" (Rose), 84
Time, 135, 140
The Tiny Rosebuds, 57, 83, 90
Tone, Franchot, 39, 120
Treacher, Arthur, 14, 17
Treasure Island Water Follies (produced by Stein), 114
Tucker, Sophie, 9
The Turn of the Century (produced by Rose), 90, 91

Ulric, Lenore, 120
"Uncle Tom's Cabin Is a Roadhouse Now" (Rose), 25
Urban, Joseph, 63
U.S. Olympic Committee, 67

Variety, 15, 16, 114, 128, 129, 135, 138
Vaudeville, 22, 45, 52, 66, 94, 132
Violins over Broadway (Rose and Anderson), 94

Waiting for Lefty (Odets), 122
Wake Up and Live, 61
Walker, Jimmy, 12
War Industries Board, 3, 30
Waring, Fred, and His Glee Club, 103
Warner Brothers, 66
Warren, Harry, 8, 14; on Rose, 6, 7
Washburne, Charles, 19
Wassau, Hinda, 83
Waters, Ethel, 87
Watts, Richard, 120
Webster, Harry McCrae, 8
Weissmuller, Johnny, 66, 68, 74; in *Aquacade* of New York, 101, 103, 107, 113; in *Aquacade* of San Francisco, 115
Welles, Orson, 140

We Will Never Die (Hecht), 124-26, 127
Whalen, Grover, 77, 80-81, 83, 84, 98, 99, 102, 112
What's in a Name? (produced by Anderson), 90
Wheeler, John, 136
"When Pansy Was a Flower," 15
White, George, 57
Whiteman, Paul, 49; at the *Aquacade* of New York, 103; at the Fort Worth Frontier Centennial, 58, 62; work on *Jumbo,* 36, 41
Whitney, John Jay, 30, 34, 35-36, 41, 45, 48
Who's Afraid of Virginia Woolf? (Albee), 139
"Why I'm Not a Legit Producer" (Rose), 121-22
Wilder, Clinton, 139
Williams, Esther, 115
Williams, Frances, 103
Williams, Hannah, 14, 15
Willie, West and McGinty, 83, 104
Wilson, Teddy, 128
Wilson, Woodrow Thomas, 3-4
Winchell, Walter, 9, 11, 19, 29; on Rose and Brice, 79
Winckler, Carlton, 52, 55, 56, 70
Wine, Women and Words (Rose), 136
Winter Garden, 28, 31
Wolpin's, 4-5, 6
"Would You Like to Take a Walk" (Rose, Dixon, Warren), 14

A Yankee Circus on Mars (Thompson and Dundy), 33
"You're in Paree" (Rose), 59
"You're So Beautiful It Hurts," 57
"Yours for a Song," 103

Ziegfeld, Florenz, ix, 8, 30, 66, 132
Ziegfeld Follies, 11, 28, 134
Ziegfeld's Roof Garden, 23
Ziegfeld Theatre, 131, 135, 136
Zimmerman, Floyd, 64, 65, 68, 70, 73